Anthropocene Poetics

Cary Wolfe, Series Editor

(continued on page 165)

Anthropocene Poetics

DEEP TIME, SACRIFICE ZONES,
AND EXTINCTION

David Farrier

posthumanities 50

UNIVERSITY OF MINNESOTA PRESS
Minneapolis
London

Poetry by Evelyn Reilly was originally published in *Styrofoam* (New York: Roof Books, 2009).

Poetry by Peter Larkin was originally published in *Lessways Least Scarce Among: Poems 2002–2009* (Exeter: Shearsman Books, 2012); *Terrain Seed Scarcity: Poems from a Decade* (Cambridge: Salt, 2001); *Give Forest Its Next Portent* (Exeter: Shearsman Books, 2014); and *Leaves of Field* (Exeter: Shearsman Books, 2004). All books and poetry copyright Peter Larkin.

Published by the University of Minnesota Press
111 Third Avenue South, Suite 290
Minneapolis, MN 55401-2520
http://www.upress.umn.edu

ISBN 978-1-5179-0625-2 (hc)
ISBN 978-1-5179-0626-9 (pb)

A Cataloging-in-Publication record for this book is available from the Library of Congress.

Printed on acid-free paper

The University of Minnesota is an equal-opportunity educator and employer.

Contents

Acknowledgments

Many things make a book: space for reading and reflection; the kindness and illumination of colleagues; and, most of all, time. In writing *Anthropocene Poetics,* I have been extremely fortunate in each respect.

I began thinking about this book during a series of wonderful, startling, and sobering conversations with my brilliant colleagues in the Edinburgh Environmental Humanities Network: Michelle Bastian, Emily Brady, Franklin Ginn, Jeremy Kidwell, and Andrew Patrizio. Our "Deep Time" reading group and the Unexpected Encounters with Deep Time workshop series at the University of Edinburgh were fundamental to my thinking about the issues discussed in *Anthropocene Poetics.* I owe thanks to everyone who came along to the reading group or contributed to the workshops on enchantment, violence, and haunting in the Anthropocene, but particularly to Michelle, Emily, Franklin, Jeremy, and Andrew, for making interdisciplinary conversations so easy and so much fun.

Robert Macfarlane kindly invited me to present a paper on Seamus Heaney in Cambridge, which set the book in motion, and Gavin Francis was good enough to travel down from Edinburgh to hear it and cheer me on. Sean Borodale and Christian Bök patiently answered my questions about bees and bacteria, and Christian generously supplied me with a copy of his unpublished poems "Orpheus" and "Eurydice." The final chapter was written during a three-month Leverhulme International Academic Fellowship at the University of New South Wales in 2017. My thanks go to UNSW for providing me with space in which to work, and I am more grateful than I can ever adequately say to the Leverhulme Trust, whose generosity allowed my family to come with me on an Australian adventure. Iain McCalman and Astrida Neimanis and their respective families provided warm welcomes to us all in Sydney. At UNSW,

Thom van Dooren was an excellent host and prompted me to think about rebounds as well as swerves, and Eben Kirksey offered valuable feedback on the chapter in draft.

Cary Wolfe and Doug Armato were supportive of the project from our first conversation. Kate Rigby offered an insightful and improving peer review, and Gabriel Levin patiently shepherded me through the production process.

It must be said that a great deal more goes into a book than even the most perceptive reader can appreciate. This one would be nothing without the influence of Rachel, Isaac, and Annie, from whom I have learned that we only truly cherish the past and the future if we live in the present.

Alex Chinneck, *A Bullet from a Shooting Star*, 2015.

Introduction

LIFE ENFOLDED IN DEEP TIME

In late summer 2015, British architectural artist Alex Chinneck installed a thirty-five-meter-tall sculpture of an electricity pylon on a patch of waste ground on the Greenwich peninsula in London. *A Bullet from a Shooting Star* was erected at a sixty-degree angle and inverted, to suggest that the pylon was embedded in the earth, having been hurled from deep space like a bolt from the heavens. The sculpture was temporary, designed to remain in place for only nine months. Poised on its tip with the great legs fanned out to the sky, it was a curiously airy, weightless image. Nonetheless, erecting it involved a sublime effort. Its foundations were 25 meters deep, and the sculpture itself was made from 1,180 meters of steel. The whole thing weighed 15 metric tons and remained upright only because of a 120-metric-ton counterweight, pointing to a cluster of terrestrial rather than celestial associations.[1]

A Bullet from a Shooting Star is a peculiarly Anthropocenic image. What would ordinarily be an unremarkable node in the web of infrastructure becomes a fabulous, even mythic injunction: an arrow pointing our attention back to the ground we stand on and that sustains us. Sited in an area where gas was once manufactured, first from coal and then later from oil, and shadowed by the financial giants of Canary Wharf, it makes our addiction to fossil fuels, the long-gestated products of very deep time, startlingly visible. Its angle of incline directs attention to our treatment of the deep past and its material traces as a resource. But if we adjust our perspective again, we can see the sculpture not as centripetal but as centrifugal, a vast cone amplifying and broadcasting traces of human presence—in the form of anthropogenic landscapes, durable materials, and altered ecosystems—to the deep future. Viewed this way, *A Bullet from a Shooting Star* becomes a conduit for deep time, a visualization of how, in the Anthropocene, distant pasts and futures flow through the present in all manner of sometimes surprising ways. Like the ribbon of stainless steel that marks the prime meridian at Greenwich, two miles away, where global time was codified and colonized in the middle of the nineteenth century, it signifies a boundary in time. Even its shape calls to mind geologists' search for the so-called golden spike that will mark the onset of the Anthropocene.

Since its rapid rise to prominence following Paul Crutzen's now famous exclamation in 2000, the Anthropocene has been deployed to name an increasingly diverse range of effects.[2] Its temporality, which asks us to accept the ethical proximity between the most fleeting act in our present and planet-shaping effects that will play out over millennia, is deeply menacing. Its breadth is bewildering, taking in Senegalese fishermen whose fishing grounds have been depleted by the changing climate, driven to make the perilous crossing to Europe in search of better prospects; jellyfish blooms so vast they flood the cooling systems of nuclear power stations; and the spread of human detritus across every environment on Earth, from the ice locked in the heart of Antarctica to the deepest parts of the ocean. Some climate scientists have sought to rein in the implication that a single term can accurately name so many different kinds of human impact on the planet's ecosystems. "The Anthropocene does not begin when humans first play 'a significant role in shaping the earth's ecosystems,'" argues Clive Hamilton. "It begins when humans first play a significant role in shaping the *Earth,* that is, the Earth as a totality, as a unified, complex system comprised of tightly linked atmosphere, hydrosphere, biosphere and geosphere."[3] Hamilton's assertion seeks to make a distinction between the ways in which humans are leaving an enduring trace that will persist into the deep future, such as the distribution of radionuclides that bear witness to nuclear explosions, and the Anthropogenically derived and *permanent* change in the way the Earth system functions.[4] His argument is for a narrow Anthropocene, determined by the findings of Earth system science, in which other disciplines, including the humanities, have no meaningful role to play.

Although mindful of Hamilton's skepticism about the term's rhetorical promiscuity, in what follows, I pursue a more inclusive approach to defining the Anthropocene, that is, that each discipline must do so according to its own terms and, by implication, that each discipline must reappraise its boundaries and assumptions in the Anthropocene's shadow. Like Chinneck's sculpture, the Anthropocene has erupted in disciplinary fields across the sciences and humanities, with unforeseen and unpredictable consequences. Mark Maslin and Simon Lewis, whose suggestion of either 1610 (and the introduction of European species to North America) and 1964 (the peak of nuclear weapons testing) as year zero for the Anthropocene is the focus of Hamilton's ire, argue that the formal geological definition of the Anthropocene must be only one among many definitions. "It is incumbent on other subjects such as history, political science, geography, etc., to have their own definitions of the Anthropocene, if," they say, "these are useful within these domains."[5] Jan Zalasiewicz, chair of the Anthropocene Working Group charged with establishing a geophysical boundary for the end of the Holocene, also suggests that "there are now many Anthropocenes out there, used for different purposes along different lines of logic in different disciplines."[6] In light of this imperative, this book considers what a poetics of the Anthropocene might look like.

Anthropocene Poetics is indebted to the earlier work of Anglophone ecocritics in the United Kingdom and the United States. Ecocriticism—the term was coined by William Rueckert in 1978[7]—has roots that go back to the 1970s, and since the mid-1980s it has achieved a steadily increasing prominence. In the United States, John Elder, Cheryll Glotfelty, and Lawrence Buell, among others, mapped its contours beyond mere writing about "nature," and in the United Kingdom, the work of the Bath Spa school, including Richard Kerridge, Terry Gifford, and Greg Garrard, established a sound basis for the more recent flowering of contemporary ecocriticism and its cross-pollination with the dynamic work of the environmental humanities. So, too, did the pioneering work in ecofeminist studies by Greta Gaard and Val Plumwood, among others, and in postcolonial studies, from

Ramachandra Guha's paradigm-breaking notion of the environmentalism of the poor to Rob Nixon's now ubiquitous concept of slow violence. By examining contemporary poetry by the light of the more recent insights offered by the environmental humanities, I hope that *Anthropocene Poetics* contributes to this tradition.

That said, the presence of such a well-developed and populated field as ecocriticism begs the question why an *Anthropocene* poetics is necessary. The sense of looming ecological crisis or the damaging influence of human activity is not new to ecocritical debates, nor are we lacking in forceful examples of transdisciplinary practice within the environmental humanities. It is tempting to co-opt Buell's famous definition of the environmental literary imagination—which posits that "the nonhuman environment is present not merely as a framing device but as a presence that begins to suggest that human history is implicated in natural history"[8]—and to assert the need for an *Anthropocenic* literary imagination. But I am mindful, too, of Timothy Clark's trenchant criticism of ecocritical work that overestimates the role of culture in behavior change. "The work of the ecocritic," he writes, "is seen as one of 'reimagination,' to change 'the imaginary' of his or her culture."[9] And yet such "suspiciously super-structural" notions risk reaffirming the problematically monolithic "we" that draws the ire of the Anthropocene's critics. I stand by the assertion that the environmental crisis is also a crisis of meaning. As Robert Macfarlane, one of the foremost advocates of an Anthropocenic literary practice, suggested, a landscape that goes undescribed also goes unregarded, leaving it "more vulnerable to unwise use or improper action."[10] But Clark's skepticism offers a necessary degree of caution. His central concern in *Ecocriticism on the Edge* is the tendency (not limited to ecocriticism, it must be said) to overstate the influence of culture and therefore of the disciplines that study it; an ecocriticism that engages with the Anthropocene will be stronger, he advises, if it cultivates a clear sense of its own limits.

According to Clark, the Anthropocene (at least colloquially) is, variously, an "intellectual shortcut," an "expanded question mark," and a "cultural threshold." These informalities make it risky, as Hamilton would no doubt agree. But they also, I would argue, describe certain affinities between rhetorical manifestations of the Anthropocene and the kind of work we often expect a poem to do. Poetry can compress vast acreages of meaning into a small compass or perform the kind of bold linkages that it would take reams of academic argument to plot; it can widen the aperture of our gaze or deposit us on the brink of transformation. In short, it can model an Anthropocenic perspective in which our sense of relationship and proximity (and from this, our ethics) is stretched and tested against the Anthropocene's warping effects.

In making a claim like this, I am reminded of Rueckert's assertion, made at the very inception of ecocriticism as a formal practice, that a poem is the "verbal equivalent of fossil fuel."[11] For Rueckert, poems, like hydrocarbons, are "stored energy," but they are distinct in that they have a renewable source in language and the imagination. Even bearing in mind that Rueckert, writing in 1978, made this comparison in the shadow of the energy crisis, such an analogy betrays a startlingly casual attitude to the finitude of fossil fuels. A contemporary gloss on this comparison couldn't avoid this or the more pressing finitude of the biosphere placed under unsustainable pressure by our consumption of hydrocarbons, and it would be shortsighted to suppose that to claim that poetry can frame the Anthropocene as we understand it today is not similarly vulnerable. So if a poem models a form of suitably Anthropocenic thinking (which I believe it does), it does so tentatively and as a means to think about poetry itself.

If we might perhaps profitably think about the Anthropocene in light of the operations of poetry, we most certainly must think differently about the poem as a consequence of the Anthropocene. In the context of Anthropocene debates about the need to revise our understanding of both deep time and the "geological status" of the human, the two principal characteristics of the lyric poem—the stability of the lyric "I" and what Jonathan Culler calls "the special 'now,' of lyric articulation"[12]—come under significant pressure. The Anthropocene involves us in a kind of deep-time negative capability, inducting us into the strangeness of a temporality that vastly exceeds both personal experience and intergenerational memory. Not every poem, of course, is about the Anthropocene or its effects. But the Anthropocene does pose significant questions about what we have come to expect from poetry since the Romantic period and therefore how we read it. As noted, the Anthropocene puts pressure on the conventional claims of lyric poetry to be governed by a singular and therefore stable (if mobile) perspective; and in *The New Poetics of Climate Change,* Matthew Griffiths argues for the particular aptitude of Modernist poetics "to articulate the complexities and nuances with which climate change confronts us."[13] Climate change may be read through Modernism and Modernism through climate change, he argues. With T. S. Eliot's famous injunction in mind, that the poet stands in relation to tradition as an agent of change and that the literature of the past must therefore be read again in light of the new work, Griffiths suggests that "we might consider the accumulation of greenhouse gases themselves a tradition; doing so would mean that climate change is usurping the role of the politicised literary scholar in bringing that history to our attention."[14] The Anthropocene must change our sense of the poem. Just as it torques the conventional priorities of the lyric, its complexities provide us with new ways of thinking about the collocation of the fragmentary and the unlikely in Modernist aesthetics.

The corollary of this is that, approached in this fashion, poetry can tacitly assist in the difficult task of approaching the Anthropocene's complex, paradoxical temporality. One of the most striking and unsettling aspects of the Anthropocene is the newly poignant sense that our present is in fact accompanied by deep pasts and deep futures. Fundamentally, the Anthropocene describes how humanity has radically intruded in deep time, the vast time scales that shape the Earth system and all the life-forms that it supports. Deep time has become both an astonishing and disorienting—and a familiar—element in the everyday. Our dependence on fossil fuels, rare earth minerals, and plastics puts us in intimate contact with far-distant pasts; the prehuman Earth shapes the present not just in terms of geological strata and evolutionary biodiversity but in terms of the textures, devices, and processes that articulate our experience of modernity. But the various ruptures that these dependencies have created—such as changes in atmospheric, soil, and oceanic chemistry and the depletion of biodiversity—also highlight our intimate relationship with the very deep future.

As Michelle Bastian has argued, the proliferation of ecological crises since the latter half of the twentieth century has left us fatally confused about time.[15] The everyday of the Anthropocene is populated with seemingly mythic entities whose temporality draws us to contemplate the prolonged presence of anthropogenic damage into the deep future— what Bastian and Thom van Dooren have called "new immortals," such as radioactive waste, PCPs, or microplastics. But in the midst of these compelling "new forms of persistence," they warn, other "taken-for-granted constancies and stabilities are breaking down."[16] As the world is being remade in the image of our desires and priorities, so our perception of deep time, and our relation to it, needs to be adjusted. It is often said that humanity has become like the meteor strike that marks the boundary between the Permian and Triassic ages. But such a dramatic, even perhaps aggrandizing comparison belies a more acute (and less flatteringly sublime) parallel. Not since the Great Oxygenation Event 2.4 billion years ago, when the rise of photosynthesizing cyanobacteria changed the composition of the planet's atmosphere, triggering a mass extinction of anaerobic bacteria and creating more than four thousand new minerals, has life so radically impacted the Earth system. The Anthropocene is an event that challenges our sense of what an event might mean. According to Bastian and van Dooren, the Anthropocene "is about foldings and pleatings, about simultaneous and contradictory temporalities, about the breakdown and (re)formulation of new multitemporal relations."[17] Similarly, Ben Dibley proposes that the Anthropocene "is the crease of time . . . the appellation for the folding of radically different temporal scales: the deep time of geology and a rather shorter history of capital."[18] If we understand the time of a poem differently, we may be better equipped to think differently about time more generally. A poetics of the Anthropocene can help us to appreciate in new ways what it means to live enfolded by deep time.

Anthropocene Poetics joins a cluster of recent work that attempts to beat the bounds of a field whose edges and points of crossing are still being mapped. Griffiths's work gives us the environmental imagination of literary Modernism. In *The Anthropocene Lyric,* Tom Bristow emphasizes place-making as a crucial element in lyric inheritance.[19] For Bristow, an engagement with the particularities of local place can expand our sense of affinity with places far distant and therefore cultivate a greater awareness of the distributed nature of what Clark calls the Anthropocene's scale effects. Sam Solnick's *Poetry and the Anthropocene* pursues the crosshatching of poetry and science and asks "what it means to read and write poetry now that humanity and its technologies have the capacity to disrupt (but not control) biological and ecological processes across multiple scales."[20] These studies have done much to show how literary criticism can respond to Zalasiewicz's proposal that every discipline must understand the Anthropocene according to its own norms (and vice versa). *Anthropocene Poetics* engages with similar questions of scale, interconnection, and response, but framed more explicitly in terms of deep time: my interest is in how our enfolding in deep time—which seems temporally distant but nonetheless erupts continually in the midst of the everyday—conjures the peculiarly wrought (and fraught) intimacies of the Anthropocene.

Anthropocene Poetics addresses the three main rubrics for understanding environmental crisis within the humanities—the Anthropocene and the "material turn" in environmental philosophy, the "Plantationocene" and the role of global capitalism in environmental crisis, and the emergence of multispecies ethics and extinction studies—to provide a more rounded perspective on this diverse, at times conflicted field. What might loosely be called "Anthropocene studies" is populated not only by the Anthropocene (in its good, bad, and ugly variations, as Simon Dalby puts it)[21] but also by the Capitalocene, the Plantationocene, the multispecies Chthulucene and its inverse the Homogocene, and the Plasticene. There are many critics for whom, even in discursive terms, the Anthropocene is a fallacy, potentially a dangerous one. Jason Moore criticizes its dehistoricizing thrust and the amnesiac inattention it encourages toward the structural factors motivating anthropogenic climate change.[22] For Andreas Malm and Alf Hornborg, *anthropogenic* is itself a misnomer for what are in fact *sociogenic* processes, driven by inequalities that are baked into the global division of labor.[23] For this strand of critical opinion, the Anthropocene naturalizes these structural inequalities. For Eileen Crist, the Anthropocene is a deeply troubling apotheosis, enthralled by "narratives of human ascent."[24] Such concerns rightly draw our attention to the risks in vaunting the role of humanity in the current crisis, as if we were both the gods and Prometheus all at once.

Yet, as Daniel Cunha has observed, the Anthropocene "is controlled neither by humanity *(anthropo)* nor by a part of humanity (the ruling class)."

Rather, "it is a situation increasingly *out* of control," a form of "domination without subject."[25] Therefore, although the order of my chapters superficially follows the arrangement of Donna Haraway's essay "Anthropocene, Capitalocene, Plantationocene, Chthulucene: Making Kin," it does so with an eye to the necessary proliferation of different understandings. Whereas Haraway's sequence is organized around a critique of the prevailing terms (Anthropocene and Capitalocene) and proposes their replacement with a more playful and multispecies-focused Chthulucene, *Anthropocene Poetics* does not privilege any one term. Rather, it advances each as a useful prism for viewing contemporary crises.

Each context forms the basis of a chapter that focuses on two or three poets. Chapter 1 looks at the "geologic intimacy" presaged by the Anthropocene in terms of the "thickened time" of lyric poetry; chapter 2 examines the extractive economies and depleted environments of the Plantationocene in the context of what Evelyn Reilly calls "relational poetics";[26] chapter 3 applies the work of Haraway and Deborah Bird Rose on multispecies kin-making to poetry concerned with a less biodiverse future.

THE POETICS OF THICK TIME

One of the defining statements on the Anthropocene within the humanities has been Dipesh Chakrabarty's assertion that humans have become "geological agents,"[27] partners with planetary systems in shaping Earth's deep future. Yet all living things are creatures of deep time, the inheritors of a legacy of infinitesimal slow change. Chapter 1 explores the intimacy that inheres within the deep time of geologic and evolutionary processes. *Thick time* refers to the lyric's capacity to put multiple temporalities and scales within a single frame, to "thicken" the present with an awareness of the other times and places. Elizabeth Bishop and Seamus Heaney demonstrate how the thick time of the lyric now allows us to imagine the complexity and richness of our enfolding with deep-time processes and explore the sensuous and uncanny aspects of how deep time is experienced in the present. Since the idea was first put forward by James Hutton, deep time has been encountered through textures and characterized by a sense of vertigo. The "geologic sublime" is almost a cliché; yet even in John

Playfair's famous, astonished remark on seeing Hutton's unconformity at
Siccar Point in 1788—"the mind seemed to grow giddy by looking so far
into the abyss of time"—there is the intimation of something even more
strange: "We felt ourselves necessarily carried back to the time when the
schistus on which we stood was yet at the bottom of the sea, and when
the sandstone before us was only beginning to be deposited, in the shape
of sand or mud, from the waters of a superincumbent ocean."[28] The rock
dissolves to sediments; as Playfair imagines himself witness to its formation, he also bears witness to rock's fluidity. In this early vision of deep
time, which has echoed ever since in the geologic imagination, a series
of transformations and breaches takes place: the lithic becomes liquid;
the weight of water replaces the weight of stone; the body is submerged
by rock and sea. Sensuous, fascinated by texture and the possibilities of
multiscalar perspective, Playfair's vision is geophiliac in its attention to
stone's mutability.

Bishop and Heaney show how writing out of an expansive sense of the
lyric present can frame an appreciation of the geologic basis of planetary
life—that life, as Kathryn Yusoff says, has a mineralogical dimension.[29]
If Chakrabarty's statement shows how the Anthropocene and its associated crises are a problem for the humanities, indicating a shift in our
understanding of what constitutes the human, the work of Yusoff and
Nigel Clark offers the possibility that life, and what it means to be human,
has always had a geologic aspect. From habitable landmasses shaped by
volcanism to the origins of culture in Neolithic art daubed in minerals on
to cave walls, we have entered our inheritance as human via our relationship with the lithic. The Anthropocene crystallizes this fact of "geologic
life," as Yusoff asserts: "'Our' geologic force is not ours alone and owes
a debt to the mobilisation of other geological materials: fossil fuels."[30] In
pursuing this line, chapter 1 engages with recent work in queer ecology
and the New Materialism, including Elizabeth Grosz, Timothy Morton,
Jane Bennett, and Quentin Meillassoux, to explore how an emphasis on
texture and the tactile in Bishop and Heaney's work frames a sense of
geologic intimacy. Looking forward to the next chapter, it also considers
the violence that inheres in relations with deep time, particularly through
Heaney's "petrocultural" poetry, in which the act of driving involves the
poems in a wider, denser web of relations defined by using fossil fuels.

THE POETICS OF SACRIFICE ZONES

Many critics have cited the absence of a structural critique as one of the main weaknesses of the Anthropocene position. Jason Moore has proposed the Capitalocene as an alternative, to account for the role of capital in forcing anthropogenic changes, whereas Anna Tsing's Plantationocene explores the legacies of colonial land use in contemporary resource extraction. Chapter 2 shows how experimental poetry allows us to see, in Moore's terms, "resources as relational."[31] Both Peter Larkin and Evelyn Reilly demonstrate how avant-garde writing can reveal the density of entanglements that lie behind ostensibly homogenized or "smooth" spaces and surfaces of plastic and plantations. Moving away from the lyric form of Heaney and Bishop, both poets explore the possibilities made available in Charles Olson's notion of the "open field" to shape a contemporary Modernist poetics of resource use. Seemingly banal Anthropocene "hyperobjects,"[32] such as forestry plantations (addressed by Larkin) or marine plastic waste (the focus of Reilly's *Styrofoam*), frequently appear to us as homogenized and shorn of relations. Yet they also have their own distinctive deep time. Tsing has shown how symbiotic relations between trees and fungi thrive even in blasted landscapes, introducing a coevolutionary perspective to commodified zones. Larkin's poetry is similarly preoccupied with the notion of "site": settings that are, he says, "compounded by the oscillations that make up the places we know, but also of those more problematic margins and creases inflecting the distance of domains we can't approach in the same way."[33] Typically, his sites are what Val Plumwood calls "shadow places" and Naomi Klein calls "sacrifice zones":[34] expendable places that can be forfeited for the sake of sustaining developed-world lifestyles. Larkin's highly idiosyncratic work, which draws on both the object-focused prose poems of Francis Ponge and the tradition of "loco-descriptive poetry," realizes the density of connections that make up what appear to be sites that are smooth or autonomous. It interrogates the ways in which forfeited spaces are "stretched and folded, . . . ribbed and reinforced."[35]

Plastic typically appears to us as disposable, decoupled from its contexts of extraction and production, yet single-use plastic may remain a lively influence on marine environments for tens of thousands of years. Any given piece of waste plastic is itself a shadow place, drifting in the currents of a vast, oceanic sacrifice zone. Reilly's work emphasizes "processes of interaction and change," to develop an ecopoetics of entangled materials.[36] Just as Olson's use of open parentheses, in Reilly's words, "made it possible to turn a poem into a theoretically endless branching diagram,"[37] her poems show how an Anthropocene perspective is characterized by an infinitely inflected, *unfolding* sequence of relations. Drawing on Moore's "World-Ecology," Tsing's studies of supply-chain capitalism, and the work of Karen Barad on diffraction and intra-action, chapter 2 proposes a diffractive poetics of entangled spaces.

THE POETICS OF KIN-MAKING

Building on Donna Haraway's thinking about kin-making between species, as well as theories of multispecies "world-making" in the work of Deborah Bird Rose, the third chapter argues that a poetics of kin-making starts with the collaborative dynamic of life itself. In terms of extinction, individual animal deaths take on a kind of spectrality: when looking upon the isolated death of an animal whose species is threatened by human activity, do we also look upon the death of that species? Van Dooren has coined the term *flight ways* to articulate this problem. Species, he suggests, are "line[s] of movement through evolutionary time," embodying a genetic and behavioral heritage that is constantly, although imperceptibly, in process; any *individual* animal is, therefore, "a single knot in an emergent lineage."[38] Van Dooren draws here on Rose's notion of "ethical time" (which she in turn adapts from James Hatley): the idea that intergenerational relations are governed by the logic of the gift.[39] To see any particular animal is also to witness the *times* that animal "ties together" along its flight way: "not 'the past' and 'the future' as abstract temporal horizons, but real embodied generations—ancestors and descendants—in rich but imperfect relationships of inheritance, nourishment, and care."[40]

This chapter presents the figure of the clinamen, the swerve, to define a poetics of kin-making in an age of hemorrhaging biodiversity. Clinamen also stands for a range of literary figures that can provide us with shapes for thinking about what a poetics of kin-making might look like: tropes such as metaphor, apostrophe, or citation all involve a turn or swerve that sets new associations in motion. Poems also have their own flight ways. If life is a form of *poiesis,* then to appreciate the depth of kin-making entanglements, we need an apocalyptic imaginary: one that can envision deep futures of world-making and world-unmaking. In formal terms, this chapter brings together the interest in the lyric and in experimental forms in the preceding chapters. In Mark Doty's "Differ-ence," the plasticity of metaphor stands for the troubling formlessness of jellyfish; in Sean Borodale's *Bee Journal,* written in the midst of Colony Collapse Disorder, the status of the lyric persona and the lyric present come under pressure in the form of a hybrid poem–journal (a form Boro-dale calls "lyrigraphs") in which composition is, increasingly, determined by the rhythms of the hive; and in *The Xenotext,* Christian Bök explores our symbiotic entanglement with microbial organisms by attempting to write an "eternal poem" in the genome of an unkillable bacterium. Each gives us a way to approach the place of an Anthropocene poetics in the greater symbiopoetic project of world-making.

Ilana Halperin, *Boiling Milk,* 1999.

1

Intimacy

THE POETICS OF THICK TIME

One overcast morning in 1999, the artist Ilana Halperin carried a small pan of milk to the edge of a sulfur spring close to the Krafla volcano fissure row, in the Mývatn area of Iceland. She knelt down and lowered the pan into the hundred-degree water until the milk began to boil. In doing so, she summoned an extraordinary confluence of different scales. Her modest act draws the domestic together with deep time, hinting at the geothermal origins of life on Earth in the nurturing associations of milk. In what appears to be a fleeting, even humble exchange between human and geologic temporal orders, a deeply Anthropocenic sensibility emerges.

Our relationship with geologic materials and processes, seemingly so remote from the scales at which human experience takes place, is in fact shaped by a deep and complex intimacy. Halperin's work is consistently concerned with making intimate sense of geologic processes. Birthdays are a recurring theme: *Hand Held Lava* (2003), a pair of short films made in 2003, the year of her thirtieth birthday, includes footage of volcanologists at work beneath Eldfell, a two-hundred-meter volcanic cone formed during an eruption in Iceland in 1973, celebrating the coincidence of their "births," and in 2009, Halperin chose her thirty-sixth birthday to crack open the last set of "cave casts" in a "geological time diptych" of stalactite formation and lava flows. The first half of the diptych consists of limestone relief sculptures formed over ten months in the hyperaccelerated calcifying springs of Fontaines Pétrifiantes in Saint-Nectaire (where the growth rate is one centimeter per year, ten times the norm); in the second, Halperin created a set of lava stamps, magma pressed between steel plates to form a seal bearing the name of a volcano and the year of its appearance, which she used to brand text-and-watercolor renderings of the emerging landscape. Each work presents deep time as peculiarly urgent, and present.

Hand Held Lava was intended, Halperin has said, to depict "slow time and fast time alongside each other."[1] The Anthropocene, similarly, represents a quickening in deep time, an uncanny coincidence of ancient resources, rapid change, and long consequence. Our intervention in the carbon cycle, excavating vast quantities of geological material and displacing it into the atmosphere, shows how this newly apparent immediacy of deep time is evident in both the material and the immaterial traces we are leaving behind. As we live through it, we encounter the deep past and the deep future in the most ordinary situations, such as through the hundreds of "technofossils"—ballpoint pens, smartphones, plastic bottles, artificial knee joints and heart valves, fiber-optic cables, contact lenses, Styrofoam cups, plastic banknotes—that surround many of us every day.[2] But deep time has always been deeply embedded in the present of life on Earth. All life on the planet is here by virtue of a debt owed to the long history in which nonlife shaped the conditions for life to flourish. The peculiar intimacy of the Anthropocene is that, in this moment thickened by contradictory temporalities and velocities, the ground has shifted. As Dipesh Chakrabarty has famously put it, we now share a geological agency with the planet.[3]

Such claims, however, have been critiqued as hubris, a vaunting assumption of privilege. For Eileen Crist, the term "crystallizes human dominion" and acquiesces to "the humanization of the Earth."[4] Anthropocentrism is a pitfall of the Anthropocene, when the emphasis is on the first part of the neologism, the *Anthropos*. In particular, the danger is that real lives are subsumed by humanity thought in the abstract, a flattened worldview that disregards the fact that the "we" of the Anthropocene is profoundly conflicted, composed of extremely mismatched orders of culpability and exposure. The experience of the Anthropocene is defined by privilege, marked by structural inequalities and huge disparities, in both consumption patterns and in the capacity to ride out the consequences of a changing climate. Furthermore, we—no matter who is included or excluded from the term—are not in control, a fallacy propounded by exponents of a "good Anthropocene"; but then, neither is this what the Anthropocene promises. Another way of parsing "the era of the human" is "the human in time": the Anthropocene has arrived bearing a pressing need to address the fact of living in a present so intruded upon by deep pasts and deep futures.

There are, as Jan Zalasiewicz has affirmed, many Anthropocenes; each discipline must reappraise its assumptions in light of its "conceptual disturbances."[5] As such, I follow Kathryn Yusoff in approaching the Anthropocene as a "provocation,"[6] a spur to the imagination to rethink and reconfigure relations in (deep) time. As explored by Bruno Latour's idea of the "parliament of things," Jane Bennett's theses on "thing power," and the speculative realism of Quentin Meillassoux, a central concern here is the reciprocal relationship between life and nonlife.[7]

Our common geologic becoming remains, of course, riven by differences. In advocating a more expansive approach to ontology, we ought not elide the distinctions made by privilege or by radically different experiences and ways of being. Rather than the totally flat field of experience and potential advocated by Bennett, in which materials are world-making agents on a par with living beings, we need to think through what constitutes the *particular* liveliness of the lithic, just as it remains vital to approach the Anthropocene not as the homogenization of an abstract "humanity" but as a reappraisal of what it means to be human in a time of political, ethical, and ecological crisis. As Gísli Pálsson and Heather Swanson observe, "a planetary that creates a sense of homogenization and oneness is not viable." Among the greatest challenges posed by the Anthropocene, they say, is "how to think scale: how to craft a planetary that itself brings difference to the fore."[8]

Halperin's work is governed by the pursuit of what she calls "geologic intimacy."[9] This is most evident in her work with body stones. In 2012, in a show called *Steine,* she exhibited stones formed in the body (gallstones, kidney stones, etc.) alongside coral samples and a fragment of the Allende meteorite (thought to predate the formation of the solar system and thus the oldest object known to science). "A body stone," she says, "is a new territory, a miniature planet travelling through an interior universe."[10] For

Halperin, they illustrate that "we as humans are also geological agents—
we form geology."[11] Body stones are organic matter within the body but
appear inorganic out of it. Blurring the boundary between the biological
and geological in this way, Halperin has identified a compellingly intimate
expression of our entanglement in what Elizabeth Ellsworth and Jamie
Kruse call the "teeming assemblage" of the geologic moment.[12]

Halperin's work describes a sympathy with the lithic that Jeffrey Jerome Cohen has called "geophilia," a condition of being enamored of the
nurturing, collaborative qualities of stone. Bedrock to the story of human
development and ballast to the human imagination, rocks are "active
partners in the shaping of worlds."[13] As with Halperin, however, Cohen's
imaginative engagement with geology is a challenge to conventional notions of what kinds of relation can yield intimacy. To handle a stone is to
make contact, he says, with a more dynamic materiality than we typically
assume: "placing your palm upon its density triggers the unexpected."[14]
In particular, it is stone's catalytic quality that engages him:

> Because of its habit of undermining human singularity, of revealing
> common materiality as well as recurring affinity, to convey within its
> materiality the thickness of time, stone triggers the vertigo of inhuman
> scale, the discomfort of familiar intimacy, and the unnatural desires that
> keep intermixing the discrete.[15]

Like Halperin's body stones, Cohen's "queerly productive" stone has the
potential to touch off in us a jolting interruption to conventional notions
of scale and relationship. The notion of a "queer ecology" imports the
troubling of the boundary between inside and outside, on which heteronormative gender strictures are based, to a rethinking of the relationship
between life-forms. "All life-forms," Timothy Morton states, "defy the
boundaries between inside and outside at every level,"[16] and in approaching
the notion of geologic intimacy, I follow the work of Cohen and Yusoff in
extending this to the relationship between life-forms and their nonliving
environments.

This chapter frames these disturbances via a complication of the
"now" of lyric address. The first aspect of what I call Anthropocene poetics that I wish to explore is the phenomenon of what Astrida Neimanis

and Rachel Loewen Walker call "thick time," "a transcorporeal stretching of past, present and future" in which our *familiarity* with deep time is recovered in the uncanny temporalities of the "uneven and multivalent" present.[17] In this chapter, I follow the prompting of Neimanis and Walker to explore the thickening of the present as a point of confluence between deep pasts and deep futures. This viscosity—devolved across species and objects, as well as the divisions of place, time, culture, ethnicity, gender, sexuality, and capital that carve up the anthropos—is the basis for a new and necessary imaginative project, a world-making for the Anthropocene, in Deborah Bird Rose's sense of becoming with others, and of Earth itself as a work-in-progress.[18] Intimacy allows us to imagine worlds of possibility; whether in terms of texture, sensuality, or violence, intimacy achieves a form of knowledge in the traffic between entities.

Poetry is world-making when it gives form to the intimacy of experience in what Jonathan Culler calls "the special 'now'" of the lyric poem. "The oddity of lyric enunciation," Culler writes, is that it presents us with a moment that is to be read and reread, "an iterable now" thick with multiple times.[19] In the work of Elizabeth Bishop, attention to the scale and texture of both geologic and evolutionary time frames is the basis for her insistence on the intimacy of detail and the queerness of boundaries. In particular, her affinity with the methods of Charles Darwin, cumulatively accruing a worldview through a wealth of glittering details, furnishes Bishop's work with a capacity to move fluently between various scales. What emerges is a poetry attuned to the way difference persists even in the midst of seemingly self-similar scenes and, as such, frames what a poetics of thick time, of intimacy with deep time, looks like. Building on this, in Seamus Heaney's poetry, there emerges a deeply sensuous engagement with geology, particularly limestone, that speaks of the depth of enfolding between human and inhuman. Heaney's lyrics are frequently thickened by other times—often drawn from the intimacies of personal memory but also reaching into much longer, geologic durations. Heaney's encounters with the geologic are often bodily or tactile, even haptic. As Mary Kinzie has observed, his eye and ear are "entrained to very particular kinds of place, texture, tone, colour, mood, weather, soil and light," such that he is able "to say how their nuances relate, almost as a geologist might."[20] But violence is also a part of this patterning of geologic intimacy. As Pálsson and Swanson observe, "dangerous geologic intimacies have long been in the houses and factories of Europeans—in the glowing red coal fires entangled with industrial capitalism and 'modern' life," to which we could add the residents of polluted or depleted extraction zones such as the Niger delta or the forests of Borneo.[21] Heaney's "driving poems," a recurring lyric position that finds the poet behind the wheel of his car, caught up in the rhythms of the road, offer an opportunity to explore what Stephanie LeMenager calls the "petroleum naturecultures" that "envelop many of us as a seamless atmosphere."[22] In Heaney's driving poems, which embroil the lyric now in a curious mix of the "instantaneous time"[23] of motorized travel and the deep timescales of fossil fuel formation and consumption that attend it, thick time is aligned with an atmosphere thickened by carbon. Bishop and Heaney each gives us an encounter with the lyric now as a particularly viscous experience, through which different times flow. In the work of each poet, we find an "invitation" to enter a "lithic alliance"[24] in the temporal torsions of the Anthropocene.

ELIZABETH BISHOP: TIME GIVES FORM TO LIFE

Before it engages us ethically or politically, the Anthropocene first presents a challenge to our sense of scale. How can its seemingly incompatible scales of action and consequence, event and outcome, and the deep enfolding of human and inhuman agencies it pronounces be given form, or even imagined? As Timothy Clark has astutely observed, the need for a critical practice capable of thinking and reading across several scales is perhaps *the* crucial requirement of an aesthetic response to the Anthropocene. "The difficulty," Clark says, "of conceptualizing a politics of climate change may be precisely that of having to think 'everything at once.' . . . Climate change disrupts the scale at which one must think, skews categories of internal and external and resists inherited closed economies of account or explanation."[25] Reading with an awareness of these "derangements of scale" will, Clark avers, both expose and disrupt structural inequalities— connecting "a patio heater in London immediately with the slow inundation of Tuvalu."[26]

Clark's call to think across multiple scales was anticipated in the work of Jorge Luis Borges. In "The Aleph," Borges describes a poet, Danieri, who aspires to write a poem of the whole Earth. Already, we learn, he has set in verse several acres of rural Queensland, a mile-long stretch of the river Orb in southern France, a gasworks in Veracruz, a commercial district of Buenos Aires, and a Turkish bathhouse in Brighton. The apparent randomness of the places already memorialized by Danieri—which vary wildly in terms of geography, population, use, and ecology—would seem to recall another of Borges's crazy lists, the famous Chinese Encyclopedia in "The Analytical Language of John Wilkins," and with it Foucault's amused reflection that such a wondrous taxonomy represents an "unthinkable space" that can only proceed through language.[27] What precisely is unthinkable here, however, is not so much the artificial proximities of language but the fallacy of holistic literary perspective. It emerges that what enables Danieri to write such distant and, for him, *unvisited* places is the presence in his basement of an Aleph, a miraculous point in space that contains within it all other points. Contemplating this node of infinite density and thickness allows Danieri to see the all in everything, as the narrator realizes when it reveals to him a disorienting chain of visions, including "convex equatorial deserts and each one of their grains of sand," a cancer in the breast of a woman in Inverness, and a globe in a closet in Alkmaar, set between two mirrors "that multiplied it endlessly."[28]

The Aleph enables exactly the derangement of scale that Clark requires of readers in the Anthropocene: impossibly enfolded, so that "the Aleph [is] in the earth and the earth in the Aleph," it assembles "millions of acts both delightful and awful," no matter how massively dispersed.[29] The most significant apparent difference between Borges and Clark is the latter's focus on deranging spatial *and temporal* scales (as per the example of "a patio heater in London connected *immediately* with the *slow* inundation of Tuvalu");[30] however, while the Aleph only permits such total vision in a "single gigantic instant," it nonetheless also enacts a derangement of time in its treatment of physical scales, or, more precisely, *textures*. As he marvels at (or suffers) the vertiginous disruptions of scale and proximity, the narrator evinces a particular regard for the textures and sensuous qualities offered by the vision: the ring of *baked mud* that marks the absence of a tree, the fineness of a hand's delicate bone structure, the viscosity of *dark blood,* and the infinite granularity from which the desert's grandeur is composed.

Bernd M. Scherer has suggested that texture can be a point of entry into the Anthropocene's strange collision of deep past, present, and deep future:

> In order to make the Anthropocene "firm," to ground it in its material, cultural, and technical substances, it seems necessary to approach it via its textures and mediations: as fluid stuff, circulating, sedimenting, leaking, crystallizing, diffusing, melting, and petrifying. As soon as we settle into a state we are shaken out of it again, excited, perturbed, agitated, toward a movement that reorganizes itself.[31]

Via their sensuous properties, certain textures can admit us to the conditions of flux that distinguish Anthropocene temporalities. It is this sensitivity to the particular that puts Borges's story in contact with the Anthropocene's distortions. Evaluations of the new world heralded by the Anthropocene require, according to Scherer et al., "a sensuous-aesthetic praxis" of scale and texture. Just as Borges can be seen to anticipate Clark's multiscalar approach, in the poetry of Elizabeth Bishop we also find a poetic form that queries the particular and the proximate so as to disrupt normative scales and worldviews. What Clark's call demands is a queering of scale, echoed in Morton's prescription for "a queer theory of ecology, which would suppose a multiplication of differences at as many levels and on as many scales as possible."[32] In Bishop, boundaries are consistently unsettled in favor of a perspective that admits what is tentative, contingent, or relational. As Anne Colwell states, Bishop "always manipulated and exploded notions of 'in' and 'out'"; for Susan McCabe, her poetry is "a site where confusion and uncertainty are allowed."[33]

Bishop has perhaps most often been read as a poet of intimacy and loss, of exacting detail and carefully achieved position, interested in the ebb and flow of relations. Victoria Harrison notes her attentiveness to "layered and changeable subjectivities" that offer "a relational subjectivity at once flexible and connective."[34] Linda Anderson observes her investment in process and tendency to "hold open the space where past and future could meet."[35] Crucially for reading a form of Anthropocene poetics in her work, Harrison argues that the "subject-subject relations" in Bishop's poetry "need not be and are often not between people, nor are they necessarily between clearly demarcated entities at all."[36] In "One Art," possibly her most well-known poem, Bishop describes loss as a daily discipline, a practice to be cultivated. The poet's accumulated losses—entities that graduate in scale from a watch to a continent—do not, she insists, constitute a disaster. Rather, the villanelle weaves together that which appears to be sundered; its rhythm and repetition insist on the persistence of relation in the face of loss.

Elizabeth Bishop has much to offer, then, to a study of Anthropocene poetics. Susannah L. Hollister has traced in detail how "the task of thinking about and across incongruous scales" was her primary poetic concern.[37] Hollister's approach is in keeping with the convention of treating Bishop as a poet whose orientation is spatial, concerned with developing her own "figurative geography," in Bonnie Costello's term.[38] However, her reflection (which opens "Questions of Travel") that "in a quick age or so, as ages go here," the rainwater staining a rock wall will become a waterfall indicates that deep time is also a key element of her thinking.[39] With the casual shrug of a subclause—"as ages go here"—Bishop indicates a sense of the familiar in the geologic that recurs throughout her work. In "Cape Breton," geologic time is legible at the scale of the very large and very small, in the "ghosts of glaciers" that have both shaped the landscape and left their "admirable scriptures" on individual stones.[40] Time in Bishop's poetry, especially the quickened sense of slow time, which figures the growth of lichen on rock as "still explosions," is "nothing if not amenable."[41] As is often the case with Bishop, in the seemingly inconsequential, echoes of far greater significance gather. The *stilled* assurance of *amenable* subtly shifts the emphasis from a linear, teleological temporality to one that is more pliable and open; its idiomatic, down-played associations also partially elide the oddness of describing time as conducive or solicitous. *Amenable* conjures a sense of accommodating, as both enframing and conceding. Time appears as both frame and reference—a force that both gives shape to and receives the impress of life. There is, therefore, a distinctive and significant temporal aspect to Bishop's examinations of scale and texture that makes her particularly useful for examining what form an Anthropocenic sensuous–aesthetic praxis might take.

In "Sandpiper," perhaps Bishop's most obviously "granular" poem, her privileging of the particular receives its most concentrated expression. The diminutive bird represents an icon of absorption, refusing to yield his attention to the boom of the much larger waves as he intently scours the surf for small invertebrates and crustacea. In an essay on Bishop, Seamus Heaney praises the "transformative" quality of her poems, most particularly in "Sandpiper": on one hand, he says, Bishop's poem addresses the compulsion to map a definitive space in the face of unsettling circumstances, anxiously attending to the shifting space between the grains of sand as the Atlantic ocean drains continually between his toes. On the other hand, though, Heaney also reads here an effort to blur distinctions, particularly of scale: "Vast words like 'Atlantic' and 'world' and indeed 'vast' itself are matched and balanced and equalled by small words like 'toes' and 'beak' and 'grains.'" The effect of destabilizing scale in this manner, he says, is to "amplify rather than narrow our sense of scope."[42] For Hollister, it "models a way to reconcile incommensurate scales."[43] Indeed, the poem affirms that the puddles of water draining between the bird's toes are *also* the Atlantic; as a good "student of Blake," his gaze finds the planetary in the particular. These readings of Bishop affirm that thinking across radically divergent scales, as the primary work of the geologic as well as the geographical imagination, is a necessary part of a considered response to uncertainty—including the terrifying uncertainties of our ecological crisis.

The bird perpetually, obsessively, searches for "something, something, something" among the "millions of grains."[44] In other words, the object of his *repetitive* search is the endless differentiation evident in the granular. What the sandpiper observes is not so much the grains themselves as their "dragging" motion, and thus what they represent: the geologic, deep-time forces of erosion and sedimentation that compose the world. Contrary to Susan Stewart's claim that the miniature represents fixity, the negation of "change and the flux of lived reality" ("the miniature is a world of arrested time"),[45] Bishop's notion of the miniature is in fact much closer to the sense of the granular as "a density that moves, circulates, shifts, translocates, and transforms."[46] From this perspective—that of the queerness of the geologic at the level of the granular—there emerges a sense of the poem that is far more concerned with the relationship between form and formlessness than with establishing a clearly defined place in the scheme of things. The poem balances form and its disintegration, the preponderance of full end-rhymes offset against the uneven line lengths, just as the occasional embedded repetitions contrast the endless, trans-formative flux in which they are set. According to McCabe, for Bishop this is a point of affirmation rather than neurosis: her work "celebrates an oscillation between constitution and deconstitution, form and formless-ness, gain and loss."[47]

In "Sandpiper," Bishop discovers the amenability of deep time, which gives form to life without enclosing it. "Time," Elizabeth Grosz says, "is the paradoxical, and perhaps unthinkable, form of interiority without itself being interior, the form of objects without being objective, the forms of subjects without being subjective or psychical, the form of matter without being material."[48] A sense of the contingency of time, and of deep time in particular, *gives form* to Bishop's poem via its engagement with flux: the shifts that take place between interiority and exteriority, the circulation of the particular within the general (and vice versa), and the transformation of longing into affinity.

"Sandpiper," then, presents an opportunity to explore the queer inheritance of scale and texture in the Anthropocene. As a poem of the minute, its companion might be said to be a poem of magnification from much earlier in Bishop's career but one similarly concerned with the shaping force of deep time. "The Map," another poem concerned with how incongruous scales can be accommodated by the imagination, also explores the slow drift and drag of geologic processes from a decidedly tactile perspective. Contemplating a map of the Labrador coastline, Bishop ponders the tactile interplay between land and sea in a version of the sensuous–aesthetic praxis espoused by Scherer, as the land embraces the sea and the bays' outlines are made available for the appreciative viewer to caress. For Hollister, the poem is an illustration of how "formal verse can contain thought not yet fitted to its structures,"[49] particularly in the way Bishop places the central unrhymed and irregular stanza between the rigidly ordered first and third stanzas, with their thudding repetends, as though in a parenthesis. A queer sensibility attends this early examination of how deep time confers form. However, whereas "Sandpiper" works with the granular to convey what Cohen calls the "queerly productive" qualities of the geologic, here she describes the implicit elimination of texture from the map.[50] In a startling inversion, the coastline of Labrador is oiled and unperturbed, with a deceptive cartographic stillness that curbs rough edges, whereas the sea is palpable and textured:

> These peninsulas take the water between thumb and finger
> like women feeling for the smoothness of yard-goods.[51]

Although they echo the mapmaker's detached, appraising manner, the women of Bishop's metaphor are also potentially disruptive, both exposing the commodifying impulse of mapmaking and disordering its masculine conventions. The smoothness conferred on the land by the map is, however, a denial of its granularity, replacing the transformative flux of the inhuman with the clean lines and distinct boundaries of a human-centered perspective. Mapping is deceptive. Nonetheless, the granular persists in Bishop's profoundly *relational* cartographic vision. Rather than a technology for creating order, Bishop's map becomes a model for the cultivation of speculative knowledge—for an appreciation of the tactile, querying (queering), and relational aspects of matter from a deep-time perspective. As in "Sandpiper," Bishop's awareness of the shaping forces of deep time, of *time's capacity to give form,* is the guiding principle of her engagement with scale.

That time gives form to life was, of course, the crucial insight of Charles Darwin. For Grosz, Darwin inaugurated a dynamic concept of time as a "becoming, as an opening up which is at the same time a form of bifurcation or divergence . . . *time as difference.*"[52] This same question of speciation, of the cumulative effect of seemingly minor differences, is the fundamental issue in Bishop's contemplation of deep time, and its contribution to defining an Anthropocenic poetics. "Considered in a very simple way," she said, poetry "is motion . . . : the releasing, checking, timing, and repeating of the movement of the mind according to ordered rhythms."[53] Time gives a poem its form in the interplay of repetition and rupture, in the tension between ordered rhythms and their variation as well as between the poem's syntax and the rhythms of everyday language. Correspondingly, her poetry continually approaches the concept that life is enfolded in the deep time of evolutionary change via her interest in the interplay of similarity and variation, and it brings together the form conferred on the poem, and the form conferred on life, in her Darwinesque attentiveness to detail.

In "Dimensions for a Novel," Bishop famously insisted on the necessity of a form that can achieve a sense of "constant adjustment,"[54] and her equally famous letter to Anne Stevenson, on Darwin, reads like a statement of artistic purpose: "Reading Darwin," she says,

> one admires the beautiful solid case being built up out of his endless heroic *observations,* almost unconscious or automatic—and then comes a sudden relaxation, a forgetful phrase, and one *feels* the strangeness of his undertaking, sees the lonely young man, his eyes fixed on facts and minute details, sinking or sliding giddily off into the unknown.[55]

Victoria Harrison reads this relatively brief, if characteristically acute, comment as a reference to Bishop's own "lifelong effort to query the unknown by reading the materials of her worlds";[56] Zachariah Pickard goes further, suggesting that a Darwinian vision of "a continuous spectrum" of gradual differences informs Bishop's poetry.[57] Her attention monitors the effect of proliferating difference, rather than resolution, that she encountered in Darwin's method of "patiently accumulating and reflecting on all sorts of facts," pursuing a formation in which "monstrosities cannot be separated by any clear line of distinction from mere variations."[58]

In "At the Fishhouses," particulars compose a world of interconnected differences. Bishop's eye leaps from detail to finely captured detail, from the thin, bright grass to the sun- and salt-bleached wooden handle of a capstan, its iron stained with rust like flowers of blood. But in a manner that recalls Darwin's refusal to police the boundaries of species and variation ("It is immaterial for us," he writes, "whether a multitude of doubtful forms be called species or subspecies or varieties . . . we see beautiful adaptations everywhere and in every part of the organic world"),

Bishop's details both collaborate in the composition of a world and stand irreducibly apart from one another.[59] "At the Fishhouses" demonstrates her recurring interest in the negotiation of like and unlike. Her insistence on the fallacy of likeness is concentrated in her observation of fish tubs and wheelbarrows coated in herring scales: "with creamy iridescent coats of mail, / with small iridescent flies crawling on them."[60] The cumulative effect of the conjunctives at the head of these lines, *with, and, with, with,* presents a world bound together by the coating of herring scales that line the tub, the wheelbarrow, even the vest and hands of the fisherman. But Bishop resists shaping these details into a naturalized series (or what Darwin called "an insensible series [which] impresses the mind with the idea of an actual passage").[61] Rather, she highlights the arbitrariness of classification. The self-similarity represented by the fish scales' fractal structure is both invoked and unsettled by the repeated adjective: what distinguishes the iridescence of the herring scales from the iridescence of the flies? Likeness, found in the peel and sparkle of light as the object shifts position, is thus refracted into something "incorrigibly plural" (to borrow from Louis MacNeice) by the repetition of *iridescent.*[62] Thus Bishop deliberately and ironically retains the friction of difference in what is apparently the poem's most self-similar moment.

It is similarly through the interplay of the same and the different that time gives form to life. Like Grosz, Morton reads Darwin as pointing to the inevitable queerness of life from an evolutionary scale, as Darwin's antiessentialism collapsed the hierarchy of distinctions presupposed by species classifications.[63] Both affirm that Darwin's famous argument in *The Origin of Species* amounts to a deconstruction of the assumptions in its title. Drawing out the analogous relationship between a deconstructive sense of text and ecology, Morton notes that "*The Origin of Species* really argues that there is no origin, just as there is no origin for text."[64] For Grosz, Darwin understood that life possesses "no real units" or definitive boundaries; the question of origin is thus "the point where Darwin's own account uncannily anticipates Derridean *différance,*" where "the origin can be nothing but difference."[65] Evolutionary time—for Morton, the deeper reality of which any single life-form is merely an abstraction[66]—thus gives a form to life in which difference persists at all scales and all levels. This folding of difference within the apparently similar matters in terms of an Anthropocene poetics, because it shows what a poetry that makes the form of deep or evolutionary time *amenable* might look like.

"At the Fishhouses" ends with a vision of liquid life that arises from Bishop's encounter with a seal. The animal appears every evening in almost the same place, a recursive moment of the not-quite-identical. Again, repetition instills a sense of difference: the freezing water is twice described as "cold dark deep and absolutely clear" and also collects a series of associations with baptism. Following the seal, Bishop imagines her own immersion in it as a transformative initiation, burning her tongue as with a Pentecostal fire. This release into language both nourishes and alienates, moving the poet from a point of putative stability into a flowing current of the unfixed and mutable, "dark, salt, clear, moving, utterly free."[67] Again, Bishop queries the privileged status of a taxonomic knowledge; flow replaces division as the organizing principle of a poem that also ends with a striking note of queered geology in the nurturing but resistant "rocky breasts" (an intimation of "the lithic in the creaturely and the lively in the stone," as Cohen puts it).[68] As Morton has asserted, after Darwin, we must understand that (from a deep-time perspective) life-forms are liquid;[69] and Bishop's work allows us to approach the question of what it means to live in the folding and unfolding of deep pasts and deep futures, in which difference is the shifting ground on which connection takes place. Difference persists; in this granular vision, the qualities of the particular (texture, depth, grain) mark the queerness of all bodies in the deep strangeness of evolutionary time and of our Anthropocenic future.

The "geophiliac" detail at the close of "At the Fishhouses" brings us back to the question of a specifically *geologic* intimacy in Bishop's work. In "Crusoe in England" and "In the Waiting Room," her Darwinian explorations of the deep strangeness of life, and specifically with volcanism, disclose a sense of what Yusoff has called "'geologic life'—a mineralogical dimension of human composition."[70] As with Halperin, both poems respond to the strange gift of volcanism in terms of the common dependence of all geologic and biological forms on Earth system processes. As Nigel Clark observes, as it evolved, life inherited an environment suited to its needs, bequeathed by the dynamism of the Earth system and the inconceivable patience and ingenuity of evolutionary time. Life, he argues, is in the gift of nonlife, but this gift also comes from a wholly indifferent source and thus arrives with a "perilous promise": the threat that what has been gifted—the conditions for life—may be withdrawn.[71]

Eldfell, the volcano that was "born" in the same year as Ilana Halperin, provides a modest illustration of this gifting. Iceland is one of the most active volcanic regions in the world: 250 eruptions have taken place in the last eleven hundred years, from hundreds of volcanoes in thirty different systems. Eldfell emerged after one of the most destructive eruptions in Iceland's history. It rose on the island of Heimaey, part of the Vestmannaeyjar volcanic system ten kilometers south of Iceland. Iceland itself is a basalt platform that sits at the junction of two large submarine physiographic structures—the mid-Atlantic ridge and the Greenland–Iceland–Faeroe ridge, the fault supplying the igneous material that continually reshapes the island. It is, in geologic terms, a very young place. The oldest rocks are only sixteen million years old.[72] The eruption that created Eldfell began at 1:55 A.M. on January 23, 1973. A one-and-a-half-kilometer fissure opened on Heimaey, suddenly and without warning. Between thirty and forty vents ejected pyroclastic material up to heights of 150 meters in the first hours of the eruption. The island's five thousand inhabitants were evacuated by fleets of fishing boats from a landscape draped by curtains of fire and continuous fountains of lava. After two days, a 110-yard-tall cone arose, which was named Eldfell (meaning "fire mountain"). Fifty cubic meters of lava was extruded in the first week. The eruption lasted longer than five months, eventually increasing the size of Heimaey by 2.2 square kilometers.

Despite the incredible power of the eruption, the town was largely saved by pumping sea water to divert the lava flow. Rather than destruction, the inhabitants of Heimaey found that, at least for the next decade or so, they entered into a distinctly intimate, generative relationship with the volcano. Residents began to return in July, not long after the eruption finally subsided. Thirty-five hundred people were back living on the island by the middle of 1974. The lava field provided the harbor entrance with a new, natural breakwater. Volcanic ash was used to extend the airport's runway. The new cone provided protection from punishing southwesterly winds. Geothermal energy heated the town until the late 1980s.

The story of Eldfell is a minor but telling illustration of how, as Clark argues, geologic processes enfold human life in deep time. In both "Crusoe in England" and "In the Waiting Room," life also emerges as intimately geologic. As if in anticipation of Halperin's speculations on the coincidence of her birth with that of Eldfell, the former opens with Crusoe's annotation of the reported birth of a new volcanic island: announced first by a tower of ash on the horizon, then by a single tephra fleck landing on a telescope's lens.[73] The dizzying turn of scale here is soon surpassed by the recollection of his own island, composed of fifty-two miniature volcanoes, each of which—in an aside that marries Crusoe the ironic Darwin with Crusoe as Gulliver—he claims he could scale in a couple of ungainly strides. Here Bishop's concern with repetition and difference takes something of a comic turn. Her Crusoe is an ironic creation, an anti-Darwin (Costello calls him a "desperate Darwin")[74] preoccupied by the *absence* of variation. His island, we are told, "had one kind of everything," a situation so stultifying to Crusoe's imagination that he recalls dying a baby goat red simply to break the monotony.[75] Reproduction is not underwritten by variation but only intensifies the homogenization of experience. Nonetheless, the island exhibits at the same a time a striking geologic fecundity: following the opening account of the birth of a new volcanic island, Crusoe goes on to describe a nightmarish vision of "infinities / of islands," spawning "like frogs' eggs."[76] This curious image of intense, *organic* proliferation condemns Crusoe to inhabit and record the monotonous flora and fauna of each in turn. Though he encounters a queered geology, then, it is one in which the immersive quality of detail numbs the imagination. "Crusoe in England" explores the consequences of *not* leavening a derangement of scales with the differentiating yeast of distinctive textures. Bishop's poem argues that in fostering a planetary sameness (like that foretold by the Anthropocene—Crusoe's island, which is his world, is an archetype for the "homogocene"), we pay the cost in the depleted possibilities for the intimacy of world-making.

By contrast, "In the Waiting Room" describes a repetition underwritten by the keen edge of difference. The poem begins, characteristically, with the local and precise: situating the poem in a dentist's waiting room, in Worcester, Massachusetts, and focalized by the nearly seven-year-old Bishop as she accompanies her Aunt Consuelo to an appointment. Left to herself in the waiting room, Bishop studies the photographs of volcanoes in a copy of *National Geographic*. Her reverie is violently interrupted by a shout of pain—which, ambiguously, could come from either the young Elizabeth or her aunt—which leads to a disquieted, even febrile reflection on the division between self and kind. As with Halperin, the volcano is central to the exploration of "queer time" in "In the Waiting Room." Costello goes so far as to call it the "central icon" in Bishop's "figurative geography." The volcano, she says, "is highly versatile, being both inside and outside, up and down, dead and alive, deep and high, solid and fluid, cold and hot."[77] In "In the Waiting Room," it is the starting point for a visionary excursion into the thickness of multiple scales.

With her gaze fixed on the magazine's cover and in particular its date (February 5, 1918), Bishop suddenly describes the abrupt sensation of falling, a vertigo so profound it is like tumbling from "the round, turning world / into cold, blue-black space."[78] Hollister has observed the impress of the *Earthrise* photograph, taken during the Apollo 8 mission in 1968, here on Bishop's imagination ("In the Waiting Room" was published in 1971).[79] Critiquing Michel Serres's celebration of the promise of the *Earthrise* image to foster a sense of cultural commons, Timothy Clark has written of the illusory holism and separateness in the conceit that it is possible to stand apart and capture the planet as a singular whole. "The Earth is not 'one,'" he insists, "in the sense of an entity we can see, understand or read as a whole." Such a false perspective denies that the Earth "is always something we remain 'inside.'"[80] We might bear in mind here, too, Timothy Luke's observation that the origin of *environment* is in the verb "to environ," which he parses as "to encircle, encompass, envelop, or enclose."[81] The implied presence of the *Earthrise* image in Bishop's poem, and the sensation of an extraterritorial plunge she describes, might then threaten to give eminence to a troublingly anthropocentric perspective, which insists upon its capacity to "environ" the Earth itself, to encircle and proscribe it within a human sense of scale. However, Bishop ameliorates this risk in the very precise reference to 1918, which gives the moment an *atomic* as well as a planetary scale. Rutherford's discovery of atomic structure in that year had at least as profound an effect on the scalar imagination as did the Apollo images fifty years later, and this destabilizing shift between the very small and the very large reflects the way the volcano, as Edelman says, undoes the central distinction between inside and outside.[82]

Just as "Crusoe in England" opens with a tale of geologic birth, the dentist's waiting room in the latter poem, charged with expectation and the mysteries of the body and occasionally interrupted by the sound of a body in pain, recalls another kind of waiting room, conjuring other kinds of generative labor. What causes Bishop's vertigo is the realization of the *unlikeliness* of likeness; that she can be both a discrete "I," an *Elizabeth,* and one of *them,* like her aunt and the women in her *National Geographic* magazine—one of a kind in both senses. But given that her epiphany of what "held us all together" is manifest as a volcanic immersion, like "sliding / beneath a big black wave,"[83] then we might also say that it crystallizes the sense that a profound otherness underwrites the human body. The shifts between different scales apparent in the poem's accommodation of the (extra)planetary and atomic apply also to the interrogative gaze Bishop turns on the notion of distinctiveness, human and individual, in the face of our coevolutionary past. The volcano points to life's origins in microbial colonies formed around nutrient-rich hydrothermal vents. As Morton insists, the lesson of Darwin is that "life-forms are made of other life-forms."[84] The riddling intermingling of viral codes in the human genome, to the point where it becomes impossible to tell the insertion from putatively authentic human DNA, illustrates for Morton that nothing has its origin outside of its environing by and interrelationship with other entities. Coevolution with microbial life has shaped the "we" we think we are in unobserved but vital ways for the duration of human history, enfolding different expressions of deep time in our bodies. In noting the depth and range of what she calls "bacterial liveliness," Myra Hird recognizes the deep strangeness we find within ourselves when we encounter our bacterial actants: all life-forms, she says, "are both ancestrally and currently, literally made up of bacteria"; in encountering bacteria, we must recognize that they "precede my relating with them . . . that 'I' am bacteria, that bacteria are us."[85]

To this end, "In the Waiting Room" brings to mind Grosz's reflection that the living body, in possession of both an "inside" (through its relation with individual variation) and an "outside" (through its relation with natural selection), should be conceived of as "a single surface or plane, . . . that is capable of being folded, twisted, or inverted, which may be seen to contain one side or another, or rather, an inside and an outside."[86] Grosz's pointedly geologic image, of the body as an uncomformity, resonates with Bishop's placement of the body at a point of inflected, enfolding scales. In both, we find a sense of the body as itself a site of shifting temporalities, where the interior and exterior relations are enfolded, Möbius-like, just as the Earth re-forms its surfaces with the interior matter thrown up by the volcano. As Edelman observes, every volcanic landscape is composed of interior matter.[87] "In the Waiting Room" demonstrates how Bishop's understanding of intimacy, as a form of invested attention in detail and scale, reveals the nature of change through the mediations of texture. Her poems describe an acute form of geologic imagination, in which we encounter the body enfolded in deep time across multiple scales.

SEAMUS HEANEY: "THROUGH-OTHER" TIMES AND PLACES

As it discloses the way time gives form to life, Elizabeth Bishop's poetry represents a site of interchange between sameness and difference, inside and outside, intimacy and detachment, body and stone. The same *traffic between* is a key feature of Halperin's work. As Andrew Patrizio and Sara Barnes, co-curators of the *Steine* exhibition, have noted, Halperin's "visual meditations on 'in-betweenness'" invite us to engage with a level of experience in which it is impossible to determine "any precise boundary between the *there* and the *somewhere else entirely,*"[88] a condition Seamus Heaney seems to have also had in mind in his reflection on what he calls "through-other" times and places.

"Through-other," Heaney says, "is a compound in common use in Ulster, meaning physically untidy or mentally confused, and appropriately enough it echoes the Irish-language expression, *tri na cheile,* meaning things mixed up among themselves."[89] Although Heaney's focus here is the mixed-up cultural and political history of the Irish poet, the echoing of phrases which suggest not only things transposed but also richly enfolded registers sympathetically with Bishop's and Halperin's efforts to trouble the boundary between the organic and the geologic. Heaney shares with Bishop what might be called a multiscalar sensibility, and, like Bishop, this sensibility is profoundly linked to a very particular experience of place.

Few poets are so closely identified with a particular time and place as Heaney, whose uneasy relation with the role of public poet during the Troubles nonetheless did not prevent his search for "images . . . adequate to our predicament."[90] According to Helen Vendler, Heaney "made his symbols a shorthand for his era."[91] More recently, however, he has been read against the more involute temporalities of the Anthropocene. Susanna Lindström and Greg Garrard propose that Heaney's negotiation of the "relationship between inner and outer environments" resonates with the emphasis on the "interdependence-yet-difference" of "biological and cultural ecologies."[92] Language, politics, memory, and the natural world meet and meld in the crucible of Heaney's lyric. With Lindström and Garrard, I believe this makes Heaney's work especially apt for thinking about an Anthropocene poetics, in particular, because these concerns are joined by a largely unremarked-upon openness to very deep time.

Heaney is typically thought of as a peatland poet, whose work describes an absorptive, even digestive relationship with place rather than a sedimentary or abrasive one. In "Mossbawn," an essay from 1978, he describes "the invitation of watery ground"; "even glimpsed from a car or a train, [such places] possess an immediate and deeply peaceful attraction." In particular, he recalls a boyhood summer evening when bathing in a moss hole with a friend became a kind of betrothal to the earth, "treading the liver-thick mud, unsettling a smoky muck off the bottom and coming out smeared and weedy and darkened . . . somehow initiated."[93] This is Heaney as Antaeus; like the long-interred Saxon woman in "Bog Queen," whose body has become "braille for the creeping influences," he receives a kind of erotic energy from the curative bog. The viscous textures and marshy territory of the bog poems typify the quality of "thick description" that is characteristic of the Heaney lyric. Peat's preservative properties also introduce an element of temporal thickening, seen in the butter that emerges still edible one hundred years after it was buried in "Bogland."

If the lyric poem in general can be characterized as an instance of condensed perspective, for Heaney this frequently congregates around the sensuous and familial preoccupations of his poetry but is also found in encounters of a more mineral nature. In "Slack," memories of the delivery of coal to the Heaney household accumulate around its specific heft and textures: the rasp of its "wet sand weight," which is nonetheless "soft to the shovel," and the "cindery skull" that formed as it cooled. We discover here an oscillation between the organic and inorganic that echoes Halperin's examination of body stones—the coal's "violet blet" recalling its vegetable origins, but also in the fact that coal's "thingness," its weight and texture, is transmuted through bodily sensation.[94] It also points to a distinctively geologic quality in Heaney's own contemplations on the lyric form. In an essay on Robert Lowell, he cites Michael Longley's distinction between igneous and sedimentary modes of poetic composition: "Igneous is irruptive, unlooked-for, and peremptory; sedimentary is steady-keeled, dwelt-upon, graduated."[95] Heaney's point is that Lowell presents a compound of both; but we might also say that his own poetry combines the sedimentary with a proneness to the unlooked-for (his observation regarding Dylan Thomas, "plunged in the sump of his teenage self" and excavating material "that would be a kind of fossil fuel to him for years to come," could equally be a self-portrait).[96] In "Slack," the sedimentation that forms the coal is rhymed with the sedimentary accretion of sense-memories, yet it ends with a rush of *"Catharsis"* like the sound of the coal "tipped and slushed" from its bag.[97]

These investigations into the familiarity of that which is distant in time in Heaney's work share the through-other quality of intimacy that is also present in his reflections on personal memory. Heaney's work returns again and again to the question of how intimacy with place is formed and sustained, particularly through sensation, "felt place" coinciding with "felt memory." It is my contention that Heaney's own encounters with the through-other qualities of *geology* also allow us to reflect on what it means to live enfolded in deep time—that reading across Heaney's output for those "shifting brilliancies" in which stone offers a passage to a more intimate relation with the monstrous unknowability of deep time.[98] Just as, as Manuel DeLanda says, "rocks hold some of the keys to understanding sedimentary humanity, igneous humanity, and all their mixtures,"[99] Heaney's by turns graduated and irruptive engagement with deep and disjunctive time scales means that his work approaches the question of what it means to be human in the Anthropocene. As it plays across multiple scales, Heaney's poetry brings up new possibilities for an engagement with the Anthropocene's thickened time.

As the most concentrated collection of Heaney's bog poems, *North* might seem an odd place to begin a discussion of what Helen Vendler has called his "stony art."[100] It is also, however, as Heaney himself said, a book "fused at a very high pressure"[101]—informed as much by a geologic sensibility as by the benediction of the moss hole. Indeed, bearing in mind Heaney's suggestion in "The Redress of Poetry" that poetry constitutes "the imagination pressing back against the pressure of reality," geologic forces appear to play a central role in his own conceptualization of form.[102]

We can see something of the congruence of the igneous and sedimentary in "Belderg," the poem that opens *North*. Heaney describes an encounter with a Mayo farmer who had recently uncovered a collection of Neolithic quernstones from the bog. Whereas bogland frequently appears to Heaney as landscape's memory, here it yields up a lattice of plow marks and the dark patterns left by Neolithic stone walls that are "Repeated before our eyes / In the stone walls of Mayo."[103] These trace fossils become images of continuity, rhyming the present farming landscape with its deep past. Like the "migrant line" of the longship in "Viking Dublin," which "enters my longhand," the line in stone issues from a sense of temporal convergence.[104] The moment is at once irruptive and sedimentary, as Heaney's attention is focused back on his own home and the "deep time" of language accessible in *Mossbawn,* a word of mixed English and Irish derivation that becomes for Heaney the root of a "world-tree of balanced stones."[105]

The careful patterning of linguistic and fossil traces in "Belderg" sketches the everyday resonances of geologic intimacy. The geologic is a common point of reference in Heaney's own domestic reflections: in "Churning Day," for example, from *Death of a Naturalist,* he describes crusts "coarse-grained as limestone rough-cast" and curds "heaped up like gilded gravel in the bowl"; in "Alphabets," geologic time parallels the time of a child's education, chalking "column after stratified column" of *Elementa Latina* on a slate board.[106] Just as Halperin's work is charged by the coincidence of her birth with that of Eldfell, for Heaney, "the fossil poetry of hob and slate," as he writes in *Seeing Things,* grounds his reflections on origins, memory, and the passage of time.[107] The trace fossils of Neolithic husbandry set up an echo with the poet's own deeply felt autobiographical traces, finding in the "familiar geologic" an expression of the "congruence of lives" across millennia.[108]

We can therefore find in Heaney a kind of sympathy with the speculative realism of Quentin Meillassoux and Graham Harman. Building on the principle, established in Heidegger's tool analysis, that objects always and inevitably withdraw from perception, Harman suggests that "things are not exhausted by their appearance to us"—that is, things possess an irreducible potential to signify that no single encounter or apprehension can ever totally expend.[109] Where the real object, whether organic or inorganic, is withheld in its essential being, in the moment of encounter, it is experienced (it "exists") as a sensual object, via its particular textures and properties. This sense of the withdrawn is a particular feature of the sense of the marvelous that the poet encounters in *Seeing Things*: "How habitable is perfected form?" Heaney asks; and yet the sensual nature of matter stands out: "rain was rainier for being blown / across the grid and texture of the concrete."[110] Indeed, Heaney seems to anticipate Meillassoux's *After Finitude* when he asks, in "Wheels within Wheels," "Who ever saw / The limit in the given anyhow?"[111] Or compare "A Shiver": to wield a sledgehammer is to know "A first blow that could make air of a wall / ... / The staked earth quailed and shivered in the handle."[112] In the eponymous "Seeing Things," meditating upon a cathedral carving of the baptism of Jesus, he notes that the sculpture's sinuous lines both represent water and constitute a complementary microscopic fluvial ecology of waterweed and water-eroded sand grains. Not only a "hieroglyph for life," the "carved stone" of water is also "alive with what's invisible."[113] Again, the through-other quality of Heaney's geologic encounters emerges: mineral and liquid "mixed up amongst themselves." If then, as Vendler asserts, Heaney pursues a "stony art" in *Seeing Things,* it is one that is also alert to what Jane Bennett has called "the shimmering . . . vitality intrinsic to matter."[114]

Meillassoux has proposed the term *arche-fossil* to describe the sense of tumbling into deep time we often experience in the presence of geologic materials. *Arche-fossil* refers not only to the fossilized traces of a past life but to "materials indicating the existence of an ancestral reality or event; one that is anterior to terrestrial life"—like an isotope of radioactive material with a half-life beyond the scope of human imagining.[115] It is, as Elizabeth Povinelli states, "the feeling of being in the presence of something that feels like it existed before us and is (thus) indifferent to us."[116] The arche-fossil is a densely entangled object, a chimera that is "substantially recomposed" in terms of its "thingness" with every new encounter. Povinelli uses the example of a trilobite, a much older fossil than those Heaney meets with in "Belderg":

> Internal to the fossil in the reader's hand is just the latest object-event in an entire series of object-events. Some of these events can be considered more dramatic changes of state than others, say as a thing such as a trilobite becomes another kind of thing such as the petrified imprint of the trilobite, which then becomes another thing such as a platform for algae in an upstate New York riverbed upon which trout nibble. . . . All are changing as they are imprinted morphically, chemically, and atomically by the absorption of their environment, and the environment too by the absorption of them.[117]

The trilobite fossil "appears" according to certain features or characteristics—its shape, density, or texture—that are activated by the senses of the individual holding it, which may in turn trigger reflections on its extreme age or the paradox between its lithic state and its lively origins. In this, the fossil is not exhausted as an object but rather recomposed according to each new event. Yet, as Povinelli observes, "Meillassoux must know that the same could be said about his own hand—the hand that grasps the fossil." That is, the hand that cradles the fossil is just as densely entangled in deep time and only appears as a "thing" when it is "abstracted out of [its] entanglements."[118]

A comparable moment occurs in "Sandstone Keepsake," when Heaney checks the heft and texture of a lump of sandstone he collected on a beach at Inishowen. The stone, which he throws "from hand to hand," is a counterpoint to his troubled reflections on the internment camp across the Foyle Estuary, at Magilligan Point in Ulster. Although this is a poem very much about the Troubles, it carries a trace of other time scales intuited in the sandstone's grain and density, carrying also "an underwater / hint of contusion."[119] "Sandstone Keepsake" is indicative of Heaney's particular *haptic* sense of the geologic encounter. In "A Postcard from Iceland," he writes of an Icelandic geothermal spring and how "that waft and pressure felt / When the inner palm of water found my palm,"[120] the consonantal inversion of "waft" and "felt" elegantly evoking the palms pressed together. As Yusoff observes, fossils help us realize "the geologic condition of the human, a reminder that our bodily composition has an originary mineralisation and a fossilised end."[121] In Heaney's arche-fossil encounters, the sense of entanglement in the geologic, what Meillassoux calls the "givenness in the present of a being that is anterior to givenness," is part of the reality of geologic life, reaching also through the body and into the most intimate spaces of everyday life.

We can think of the Neolithic reflections in "Belderg," then, as a kind of point of entry into thinking about Heaney's geologic intimacy—a "door into the dark" of even deeper time. The stepping-stone is also an important image of passage. In "Something to Write Home About," he states, "The stepping stone invites you to change the terms and the *tearmann* [terminus] of your understanding; it does not ask you to take your feet off the ground but it refreshes your vision by keeping your head in the air and bringing you alive into the open possibility that is within you."[122] This is perhaps most evident in *Seeing Things,* a hinge collection through which, as Heaney himself acknowledges, he learned "to credit marvels."[123] In the first two poems in the sequence "Squarings," he describes taking possession of his cottage in Glanmore: it is a place at once motile and grounded, home, as he says in "Glanmore Sonnets," to both "the marvellous and [the] actual."[124] In the first poem, "the soul-free cloud-life roams" in rainwater puddled in the empty hearth; in the second, his attention turns subterranean: "Sink every impulse like a bolt."[125]

As Vendler has observed, in *Seeing Things,* Heaney pursues "two orders of knowledge," the marvelous and the phenomenal. It is a collection, she says, in which "the imagination must work to set mobility of mind against the immobility of the inhuman."[126] This perspective connects Heaney's work with what Nigel Clark calls the monstrously inhuman aspect of very deep time. Anthropogenic climate change, Clark says, puts social thought in contact with the true nature of our gift relation with the "fully inhuman" planet on which we depend—a relationship in which a corresponding countergift is unthinkable.[127] What this requires, Clark says, is "a new willingness in critical, social, cultural, and philosophical thought to embrace the fully inhuman, in all its variability and volatility."[128] In "Lightenings X," Heaney contemplates a cliff face that overhangs water in a Wicklow granite quarry. The pool, decorated with the reflection of "cargoed brightness travelling // Above and beyond and sumptuously across," might qualify as an image of the "mobility of mind" and the cliff's "Stony up-againstness" the "immobility of the inhuman" that Vendler reads as opposing forces in *Seeing Things*.[129] Yet the poem focalizes not the polarization of the geologic and the liquid but the *reflection* of the massive in the diaphanous. The scene takes on a kind of through-other quality, an expression of the "unlooked-for" liquidity of deep time. This is not only because Heaney alludes to Tennyson's Lyellian reflections in *In Memoriam* ("the hills are shadows, and they flow / from form to form, . . . / like clouds they shape themselves and go") but because the crystals that stud its surface also glint with the memory of the Wicklow Mountains' origins beneath the tropical water of the Paleozoic Lapetus Ocean.[130] Like the threading of the marvelous and the phenomenal that occurs throughout the collection, the conjunction of diaphanous rock in massive water produces stepping-stones for the imagination, toward the astonishing discovery of the gift relationship with unimaginable deep time on which human existence depends.

Other poems in *North* provide evidence of a geologic intimacy of a more erotic cast. Whereas in "Belderg," we have an expression of the lithic in communion with the familiar and homely, "Bone Dreams" explores a more sensually charged encounter in which the "rough, porous / language of touch" of a white bone picked up in a field builds into a dreamlike, erotic encounter. The poet-paramour ossifies himself gazing upon the prone form of a lover whose body becomes a chalk landscape to caress and explore, and *possess*. The dreams (or nightmares) of empire are never far away in *North,* and here a far less comfortable intimacy replaces the familiarity discovered in "Belderg." Rather than a trace fossil, here we have the moment of death—a white bone—but connected to life via the "little death" of orgasm. Heaney's "geologic erotic" is conflated with imagery of domination and desire, inscription and incursion. This dream also features a dizzying series of contractions and expansions of scale: Alice-like, the poet variously is dwarfed by and towers over the landscape of his lover's body. "Bone Dreams," which ends with Heaney touching "distant Pennines" in the spine of a dead mole, is further indication of his haptic approach to deep time. In the erotic expressions of conjunction, porosity, and the surrender of boundaries in Heaney's geologic intimacy, we can productively think through some of the temporal and spatial conjunctions of the Anthropocene. The poet's transformation into a "chalk giant" in "Bone Dreams" shows how geologic intimacy, especially via his investigations of the more porous, motile formations of calcium carbonate, can also be motivated by erotic energies and productive of multiscalar temporal perspectives.

Calcium carbonate landscapes are often associated with queerly mutable and desiring bodies. Alice Oswald writes of "chalk with all its pits and pores, / winter flowers, smelling of a sudden entering elsewhere" in *Woods, Etc.*[131] Tim Robinson also links this to limestone's malleability, as seen in the phenomenon of mammillation, whereby weathering and acidic erosion produce a "curiously organic undulating surface" in this "so readily eroticized rock-surface."[132] Perhaps the most striking instance is Auden's "In Praise of Limestone," which meditates on its markedly sensual geology. Because it "dissolves in water," limestone, Auden says, is "a stone that responds." Edna Longley has identified a subterranean transcorporeal narrative in this poem, in which "limestone also takes on the contours of the male body 'entertaining' its lovers and itself." Resembling both water and stone, limestone possesses a friability that, Longley says, "questions fixed boundaries," including its own "androgynous gendering."[133] As such, limestone's "inconstancy" invites us to read it as an instance of the transformative potential of a kind of queer mineralogy.

The mutable and motile sensibility of Auden's poem, with its reflections on the processes by which organic matter becomes inorganic limestone and nature transforms into art, anticipates Yusoff's recent investigations of what she calls queer geology.[134] In a discussion of the birdman painting in the limestone caves of Lascaux, dated to between seventeen thousand and twenty-two thousand years ago, Yusoff proposes that we need to understand the origins of the human *in geology*: "Prehistoric geomorphic aesthetics," she says, "offer a passage into thinking a mixed inheritance . . . which includes the geologic within its purview as constitutive of identity."[135] Yusoff queers the common assertion of the Paleolithic Lascaux paintings as an originary moment in the development of human consciousness:

> The human in Lascaux cannot be human alone without the profusion and exuberance of nonhuman life and its community of being. . . . Always there is the presumption that it is "Man" who touches rock, but is it not the rock that touches Not-Man into being? Is it not the rock that lures the waiting imagination to find something that subtends it? . . . The image depends on geology, on how the mineral holds and paints the image, on how the shifts from glacial to interglacial seal the cave to guarantee its endurance beyond the present of its inscription.[136]

Like Halperin's body stones, the boundary between organic and inorganic dissolves in the feldspar, hematite, limonite, charcoal, and magnesium dioxide paints used by the prehistoric artists and in the absorptive qualities of the limestone surface that holds them. As with Nigel Clark's reflections on humanity's gift relation with the monstrously inhuman, Yusoff here extends what Rosalyn Diprose calls corporeal generosity to include "the inhuman . . . within the very composition of the human."[137] Her reading opens up the tactile, queer possibilities in moments of thickened time and therefore in the formulation of an Anthropocene poetics.

A comparable encounter occurs in "On the Road," from the "Sweeney Redivivus" sequence, which imagines a descent into the Lascaux caves as a kind of refuge. Descending to the deepest hollows, Heaney discovers an image of a drinking deer carved into the cave wall. The muscles of its body swell in concert with the contours of the rock, flowing zoomorphically and geologically from haunch to head as the depicted animal strains, in the manner of Keats after the Grecian urn, to reach "a dried up source."[138]

Heaney's engraved deer lies in a chamber known as the Apse, only a few meters from the birdman of Yusoff's reflections. It invokes some of the same curious temporality of what Yusoff calls the "geologic now":[139] the rhyming of the animal's upper body with the cave's contours suggests an intimate sympathy of form, which echoes the implication of rhymed "spots of time" in the moments of composition and reflection. But this also contrasts with the image's ineluctable untimeliness—separated by millennia but bonded in the perpetual urgency of the straining, expectant tongue. To go into the rock in this way is also to enter a deep time intimacy, via a kind of through-otherness: as it picks out the limestone's contours to reveal the deer's shape, the confluence of a human-imagined animal outline and stony contours becomes a "knot of time," summoning the inhuman inheritance within the human.

Significantly, "On the Road" begins as one of a small number of driving poems in Heaney's oeuvre, a fact that consolidates its relationship with a queer geology and thickened time. For Heaney, participating in petroculture is a deeply affective, sensual experience,[140] involving what Jack Katz calls the capacity to "embody and be embodied by the car." According to Katz, the driver feels

> the bumps on the road as contrasts with his or her body, not as assaults on the tires, swaying around curves as if the shifting of his or her weight will make a difference in the car's trajectory, loosening and tightening the grip on the steering wheel as a way of interacting with other cars.[141]

Likewise, in "On the Road," Heaney grips the steering wheel "like a wrested trophy," while the road reels steadily beneath him. Driving thickens the present with other times and places: "The trance of driving / made all roads one," as Heaney remarks.[142] In "Postscript," one of several poems to describe a journey through the limestone landscapes of the Burren in County Clare, Heaney describes a through-other scene that exults in the motorized encounter. Driving along the shore road with the ocean to one side and a lake to the other, he is arrested by the sight of a flock of swans like "earthed lightning." Echoing Yeats's nine and fifty swans, Heaney acknowledges that the truly marvelous aspect of the scene will elude him: "Useless to think you'll park and capture it / More thoroughly."[143] Yet, contrary to Jonathan Bate, for whom the presence of cars in Heaney's poetry signifies containment, an inability to enter the "wild" outside,[144] including the car in an otherwise pastoral scene illuminates the fallacy of a separate "nature." Heaney's experience in the car is as a conduit for the uncanny and intimate, "neither here nor there, / A hurry through which known and strange things pass"[145]—not separated from the scene but drawn into a thicker time of interobjectivity in which, as the destabilizing momentum of the buffeting winds meets the counterpointed momentum provided by burning the remains of carboniferous life-forms, the poet's heart is caught off guard and blown open.

As with Yeats's observation that the Coole swans will build among the rushes of another, distant pool, in "On the Road" and "Postscript," the sense of something withdrawn sits alongside the stepping-stone change in the poet's understanding. In "The Peninsula," Heaney resorts to his car when he senses language itself withdrawing from him. Here the driving poem describes an effort to outpace form and move beyond language to a kind of fluidity that resists purchase, a landscape you do not arrive in but merely "pass through" to the discovery of "thingness," "The leggy birds stilted on their own legs, / Islands riding themselves out into the fog." The poet turns for home, still silent, but now instructed in the art of decoding places by means of "things founded clean on their own shapes."[146] In "Ballynahinch Lake," paused during a drive through Connemara, Heaney discovers that the sense of something withdrawn can also be a point of passage into a more thickened temporality. In a moment that recalls the earlier through-other entry of cliff and pool into each other, the mountain's reflection in the lake is a "captivating brightness" that "Entered us like a wedge knocked sweetly home / Into core timber."[147] And as with "Postscript," the sight of a pair of water birds prompts the poet to reflect on the scene's uncanny intimacy: "something in us" is "unhoused" by the birds, before the firing ignition shakes them back to themselves.

The uncanniness of the moment is only partly due to the "trance of driving," however. Stephanie LeMenager notes that the "petroleum infrastructure" that sustains the car has become "embodied memory and habitus for modern humans."[148] LeMenager emphasizes that affective embodiment of the kind Heaney experiences behind the wheel extends beyond the individual driver. Mimi Sheller and John Urry have also observed how driving constitutes a kinesthetic intertwining of "motion and emotion," produced through "a conjunction of bodies, technologies, and cultural practices."[149] Driving situates the driver at the center of a "powerful machinic complex" with an exemplary temporal and spatial reach,[150] taking in the deep past of the fossil fuels that power the car and the chemically altered planetary atmosphere it contributes to; the mass displacement of geologic material that has led to the production of enough concrete to coat one kilogram over every square meter of the Earth;[151] and the emergence of extractive economies that despoil and pollute, creating sacrifice zones out of both oil fields and the lungs of those who breathe their toxic fumes.

In "Oysters," Heaney arrives at the coast having again driven across the Burren limestone. It is a strikingly sensual poem that sets up a troubling theme of consumption and violence and the sedimentation of deep time: the bivalves, "Alive and violated / ... on their bed of ice," echo in the carboniferous landscape Heaney crosses.[152] Furthermore, the animals' relation to deep time is as queer as that of the limestone they are rhymed with. As Rebecca Stott has observed, oysters represent both fixity and fluidity: on one hand, the oysters Heaney eats in the poem would have been virtually unchanged from oysters that lived more than 200 million years ago and gave their shells to build the Burren landscape; on the other, they are "the most prolific and sexually fluid" of marine animals.[153] Oysters have evolved to begin life male but mature as female and can change sex up to four times a year depending on changes in water temperature and salinity.[154] Heaney finds echoes not only between bivalves and the Burren but also between his own journey and that of the Romans who hauled their own oysters from the coast of Brittany. His motorized journey through the limestone landscape is thus a spur to a further encounter in which human violence is crossed with the queerness of deep time. "Oysters" shows how journeying across deep time can also throw up unwelcome connections— of the structural violence of Empire and the "Glut of privilege."

Heaney's driving poems entail a mass displacement of scales; although he rarely directly acknowledges the material facts of petrocultures, the fact that his driving poems are so often points of entry to a sense of displacement or disorientation conjures an Anthropocenic sense of thickened time. However, his reluctance to trouble further the "seamless atmosphere" in which we are enveloped by what LeMenager calls "petroleum naturecultures" limits what his poetry has to say about being Anthropocenic.[155] "Geologic life" is more than the wonder of mineral inheritance; as Yusoff explains, "we have only to think of the difference in life expectancy between the fossil fuel rich and poor to understand that the potential of a body to be what it is is conditioned by the fossil fuels that it can incorporate."[156] As I explore in the next chapter, an Anthropocene poetics must take account of where geologic intimacy tends toward violence.

Life has always been geologic; understanding this is a necessary step to achieving an appreciation of what is distinctive about the Anthropocene, in which humanity is newly encountered as a "geologic agent." The Anthropocene is not a sudden and novel alignment of human life with the lithic but the unbalancing of an ancient equilibrium, a usurpation of influence, and a distortion of scales. Bishop's and Heaney's works show the capacity of the lyric poem to express this peculiar thickening of times, framing an Anthropocene poetics in which multiple other times—both distant and available—flow through the "now" of the poem. If Bishop's poems help to engage a form of geologic imagination, in which the body is enfolded in deep time, Heaney's work allows us to approach the Anthropocenic dimensions of this. His "driving poems" engage with the extrapolated reality of what Morton has called the hyperobject: an entity "whose primordial reality is withdrawn from humans."[157] Hyperobjects can be topographical, material, or structural ("the Lago Agrio oil field in Ecuador, . . . Styrofoam . . . , or the sum of all the whirring machinery of capitalism" are some of Morton's varied and vivid examples),[158] but a key characteristic is what he calls their "viscosity"—the way in which they are both *indicative of* and *experienced in* the "thickening" of time.

Hovering behind this, however, is the violence that underpins much of our "geologic becoming." Drawing on Richard Dawkins's extended phenotype, Morton illustrates this with another startlingly Heaneyesque image: "When I pick a blackberry from a bush, I fall into an abyss of phenotypes, my very act of reaching being an expression of the genome that is not exclusively mine, or exclusively human, or even exclusively alive."[159] "Blackberry Picking" is a sensuously viscous poem, from the heavy weather that ripens the "glossy purple clot" of the blackberry to the glorious experience of eating the first sweet fruits of the season, "Like thickened wine"[160]—viscous, too, in the way in which it draws Heaney into a thickened temporality. From a deep-time perspective, Heaney's recollection of blackberry picking and the childish disappointment at organic decomposition becomes a confrontation with what Morton calls "the abyss in front of things"—in this case, the common heritage of the Great Oxygenation Event more than 2 billion years ago, a cataclysmic moment for anaerobic bacteria that was nonetheless the basis for life as we know it today. The fungus blemishing Heaney's blackberries is botrytis rot, a necrotrophic fungus that produces an oxidative enzyme. Thus out of the abyss of deep time, the mitochondria in his cells, which provide the young Heaney with the energy to collect his "lovely canfuls," connects him both to their oxidative spoliation and to the early cyanobacteria that ended the dominance of anaerobic life on Earth—back, even, to the hydrothermal/mineral origins of the earliest forms of life. If reading "Blackberry Picking" in the Anthropocene illuminates the depths of our geologic intimacy, it also calls us to reflect on the parallels between planetary ruptures past and present. These ripples in time extend an apparently simple action, such as reaching to pick a blackberry, to a past extinction event, through the *sensuality* of deep time, in which we can discover the depth and richness of our enfolding in geologic intimacy.

Julia Barton, *#LitterCUBE*, 2015. Strapping, polyethylene terephthalate PET or PETE, woven assemblage, 15 × 15 × 15 cm.

2

Entangled

THE POETICS OF SACRIFICE ZONES

In the titular essay in her collection *Findings,* Kathleen Jamie describes being forced by poor weather to abort a planned trip to St. Kilda and divert to the Monarch Islands off the western shore of North Uist, Scotland. St. Kilda, famously, is an icon of the enduring possibilities of the wild and abandoned, imagined as a site purified of human influence. On the beaches of Ceann Ear, however, Jamie discovers a strikingly entangled scene. Combing the beach for objects that might describe something of the pull of wild places, Jamie and her companions discover an astonishing collection of objects at the wrack line: paintbrushes, exhausted rolls of masking tape, shampoo bottles, and abraded lengths of tangerine fishing net. "We knew their shapes," Jamie remarks, although they were faded and slipped of their labels.[1]

This assemblage of marine debris spurs a kind of epiphany. The banal items so obviously out of place possess a fascination that is peculiarly their own. In part, it is the surprise of connection, of familiar things washed clean of their histories and set down in an unfamiliar setting. She also discovers a whale's carcass and wreckage from a light aircraft, lending the scene a tinge of both catastrophe and the fantastic; and, aware that it implies a false disparity, Jamie reflects on the misleading randomness: "Here in the rain, with the rotting whale and wheeling birds, the plastic floats and turquoise rope, the sealskins, driftwood and rabbit skulls, a crashed plane didn't seem untoward. If a whale, why not an aeroplane? If a lamb, why not a training shoe?"[2] The point is that the urge to see distinctions is rooted in an urge to simplify—to impose an order and regulate what belongs and does not belong. "We can't make distinctions about what to admit, about 'good' and 'bad' nature," she has said elsewhere. "The plastic of your pen has its resource in oil, which is part of the natural world. The breast milk of polar bears has chemicals in it. There is nothing untouched. To hanker after the truly wild is a fantasy."[3]

What Jamie discovers on Ceann Ear is what Val Plumwood calls one of the "shadow places of the consumer self," a site where the material conditions that enable twenty-first-century life are smoothed over or suppressed.[4] Naomi Klein calls them "sacrifice zones": places, such as oil fields or opencut mines, that are sufficiently out of the way of consumer experience or where the rights of inhabitants (typically indigenous or nonhuman) are held sufficiently lightly that they can be considered expendable. "Fossil fuels require sacrifice zones," Klein said. "They always have. And you can't have a system built on sacrificial places and sacrificial people unless intellectual theories that justify their sacrifice exist and persist."[5] The logic of sacrifice zones isn't limited to fossil fuels but rather is endemic to the particular means of organizing nature that Jason Moore identifies as inherent in capitalist world-ecology.[6] The division of the world into inventory or surplus has led to an immense dispersal of sacrifice zones, on scales both large and small, from Indonesia's 6 million hectares of palm oil plantations to the estimated 100 million metric tons of plastic debris, most of it in microscopic fragments, that constitute the five Pacific and Atlantic garbage patches. But for all their ubiquity, to many in the developed world, sacrifice zones exist beyond the horizon of perception—in Jacques Rancière's terms, they do not disturb the distribution of the sensible.[7]

The geological intimacies explored in chapter 1 demonstrate how an Anthropocene poetics is, in part, a matter of intersecting orders of difference—fast and slow, great and small, deep and shallow time interacting in and through human action to shape the world that also, in turn, shapes us. But an Anthropocene poetics must also examine the deeply relational composition of capitalist world-forms that present the world as homogeneous, simplified, and autonomous. The denial of complexity is the common denominator to every sacrifice zone. Arranging nature in the interests of capital requires a mass simplification: the reduction of all life into the categories of resource or waste. Sacrifice zones, or shadow places, purport to disentangle the web of life, offering smoothed edges and managed inter-actions in place of the "intimacy, porosity, and permeability" that, Moore says, mark the coproduction of all natures in "the relation of life-making."[8]

Jamie's reflections on Ceann Ear restore some of the sense of entanglement to a scene that would otherwise quite readily lend itself to the smoothing effects of the landscaping eye. Scottish artist Julia Barton has also found means to illuminate the complexity embedded within sacrifice zones. As part of ArtCOP21, a global festival of artistic responses to the Paris Conference, Barton sought a way to visualize the volumes of plastic waste she had found washed up on beaches around Scotland and the waste energy they contain. Barton gathered marine plastic debris from five beaches and sorted it into five types: corrugated polypropylene sheets (used to construct prawn boxes), polyethylene terephthalate (PET) strapping (used to hold prawn boxes together), polyethylene mussel pegs, polypropylene tubes (the shafts of cotton buds), and strands of PET mixed microfibers (used to make ropes and plastic bags). Each type of plastic was then stacked into a cube, measuring five to twenty cubic centimeters, alongside which Barton itemized its "embodied energy content": the amount of energy it contains, from the raw materials to the costs of extraction, manufacture, and transportation.[9] The resulting artworks, each one called CUBE, give material shape to the deep time embodied in seemingly ephemeral plastic. The polyethylene strapping used to hold together the fish packaging boxes that constitute one CUBE, collected from Dun Canna beach in Ross-shire, contained the equivalent of 0.36 liters of petrol, or 11.81 megajoules per kilogram; the polypropylene boxes themselves, by contrast, contained 3.72 liters of petrol, or 122.1 megajoules per kilogram.

The CUBEs combine a sense of weightlessness with the monumental. In particular, the stark whiteness of the CUBE depicted at the head of this chapter conjures both a haunting, spectral impression and, at the same time, a tangible, forceful density. The low angle of the photograph creates a brooding, glacial quality and a disorienting sense of disrupted scale, as if it had calved from a great iceberg; the busy tangle recalls images of bleached coral. As such, it becomes a kind of ghostly monument to the future we are creating—an uncanny marker of what is to come, looming out of deep time—while at the same time calling to mind the density of inextricably interwoven lifeways that are being unpicked in the Anthropocene.

Barton's neatly stacked CUBEs elegantly convey the entanglements that sustain what so often appears to us as a simplified world. Anna Tsing's term *plantationocene* describes how the ways of organizing nature innovated by the plantation system have become endemic. The colonial sugar plantation was a sacrifice zone, in which the only valued life was that of the commodity. Plantations coupled a genetically isolated, cloneable planting stock with an equally isolated and replaceable source of enslaved labor and an ideology of *terra nullius* to design a way of organizing nature that could be replicated in different environments across multiple scales without dissenting from the original basic design. *Scalability,* Tsing says, systematized a particular way of seeing the world as radically simplified into a fund of exportable resources: "to see only uniform blocks, ready for further expansion."[10] Meaningful diversity is banished; "everything else becomes weeds or waste."[11]

Both plastic and plantations are examples of the way scalability shapes our interactions with the world around us. But these apparent sites of simplification also, as this chapter demonstrates, reveal a lively and irreducible entanglement. In what follows, I argue that Peter Larkin's investigations of English plantation forests and Evelyn Reilly's examination of the liveliness of plastic in her collection *Styrofoam* offer a kind of diffraction-based poetics that renders visible the dense entanglements underlying the simplified world.

Karen Barad has proposed diffraction—the effect of differences in phase and amplitude between overlapping waves—as a way to observe the emergence of entangled phenomena. Whereas reflection represents a merely solipsistic form of knowledge, diffraction patterns "map where the *effects* of differences appear."[12] Whether of sound, light, or liquid, waves are not things but disturbances in a medium and can therefore overlap at the same point in a phenomenon called *superposition.* In quantum physics, diffraction is related to the capacity for light to behave in a particle- and a wavelike manner simultaneously: the *dual wave–particle paradox.* For Barad, diffraction patterns are "patterns of difference that make a difference" because they "make evident the entangled structure of the changing and contingent ontology of the world."[13] That is, diffraction exemplifies what Barad calls *intra-action,* the collaboration of distributed agencies engaged in making environments. Whereas Larkin's decades-long obsession with forestry plantations exposes the relationality that is exploited but not exhausted by agricultural monoculture, Reilly's *Styrofoam* describes polystyrene in particular and plastic in general as what Jennifer Gabrys, Gay Hawkins, and Mike Michaels call a process of "transformative material engagements."[14] Each produces work that creates diffractive patterns of overlapping difference: Larkin's "coppiced" verse—marked by permeable networks—and Reilly's polymerized chains of association allow readers to appreciate the dense entanglement of entities that appear at first to be bounded by a reducing logic of scalability.

PETER LARKIN: HOW DO INDUSTRIAL FORESTS THINK?

According to Eduardo Kohn, forests can think. Drawing on the inclination of all living things to form habits—to adapt to the circumstances and exploit the opportunities presented by a given environment—Kohn suggests that this pattern forming is "what makes life as a semiotic process."[15] All life-forms are continuously engaged in appearing to one another in a process of sign making. Thinking is therefore not limited to the human, Kohn asserts; nor are signs "exclusively human affairs." As life-forms "read" and respond to the habits encoded within the environments they live in and the other species they share them with, they adopt or adapt, and thus amplify these habits.[16] In this sense, evolutionary adaptations are unconscious interpretations of the world that pass, through the animal's or plant's bodily interaction with its environment, into an intergenerational signifying process. "The specific shape of the anteater's snout" is a sign, Kohn says, "to the extent that it is interpreted . . . by a subsequent generation with respect to what this sign is about (i.e. the shape of ant tunnels)." The interpretation is manifest in the body of each generation of anteater, creating "a new sign representing these features of the environment." Ant, anteater, and tunnel collaborate in a signifying process: "The logic of evolutionary adaptation," Kohn concludes, "is a semiotic one."[17]

Kohn's argument involves a radical expansion of the way signs are made. In addition to the signifier and signified, he states, signs possess meaning in relation to a "somebody"—and this somebody, for Kohn, need not be human. Kohn's organic semiosis extends selfhood to all living things. Selfhood does not stand apart from but emerges *within* the semiotic process. Because selfhood emerges through the process of "maintaining and perpetuating an individual form" that "grows to fit the world around it" without losing its distinctive edge of difference, Kohn is able to posit the forest as "a dense, flourishing ecology of selves," an echo chamber of multispecies thoughts and signs amplified into the future.[18] Kohn has shown how Barad's concept of intra-action is manifest in the "semiotic" life of a tropical forest. A forest thinks through the countless intra-actions that foster biodiversity; how, then, does an industrial, *monocultural* forest think?

The industrial forest, from an Indonesian palm oil estate to an overlooked clump of commercial pine in a British field, is a contemporary manifestation of the plantationocene. James Scott attributes this particular mode of seeing the world to the invention of scientific forestry in late-eighteenth-century Prussia and Saxony. Anticipating Moore's insight that capitalism is a way of organizing nature, Scott proposes that government through simplification reduced the Crown's interest in the forest to a single number or bottom line: the revenue that could be extracted from it. In this way, "the whole forest could be taken in a single optic," that of *profit,* and, "at the limit, the forest itself would not even have to be seen; it could be 'read' accurately from the tables and maps in the foresters offices."[19] This "great simplification"—plants become "crops" or "weeds"; insects become "pests"—synthesized the teeming mass of lifeways represented by "the forest" into a "one-commodity machine."[20] As Peter Larkin puts it in "Three Forest Conformities," "we environ the mean / kernel of nature,"[21] glancing, perhaps, at Timothy Luke's observations that "to environ" will always entail "a strategic disciplinary policing of space."[22]

However, for Tsing, the irony of "salvage accumulation," the creation of value by stripping entities of all their nonscalable properties and contexts, is that it "reveals a world of difference."[23] Capitalism only symbolically severs the unruly entanglements of intergenerational species–environment coproduction. In reality, it creates, in Moore's words, a "denser, more geographically expansive, and more intimate" series of enmeshments, in which capitalism internalizes the biosphere and the biosphere internalizes capitalism.[24] Tsing's iconic example of unruly nature is the matsutake mushroom, a luxury food commodity that "cannot live without transformative relations with other species." Matsutake are the fruiting body of a subterranean fungus. They are ectomycorrhizal, which means they form symbiotic relationships with the roots of particular plant species, typically pines, which are grown as plantation stock and often persist in the ruins of former industrial forests. As a luxury food, matsutake are exchanged around the world for high prices, often far from the sites where they are harvested, through global supply chains. The mushrooms exemplify, for Tsing, the way in which supply chain capitalism doesn't eliminate difference but rather appropriates it. Matsutake move in and out of registers of the scalable and nonscalable; the mushroom "begins and ends its life as a gift," existing as inventory for only the few brief hours between harvesting and sale. Its scalable property, that is, its retail value, is indivisibly entangled with the "transformative mutualism" of its relationship with the roots of trees that it both draws nutrients *from* and provides nutrients *for*.[25]

Both Moore and Tsing offer perspectives that dissent from the image of a simplified world of inventory and surplus. Similarly, Larkin's renderings of seemingly bounded spaces reveal the way that these processes of simplification divorce the commodity form from the rich, entangled contexts of world-making that produce it—entanglements that involve the deep timescales that shape the multispecies, collaborative flourishing Kohn defines.

The modesty of Larkin's subject—small, easily overlooked, and unpeopled clumps of woodland in the English midlands—might seem rather removed from the violent externalization of nature in the plantationocene. But his work is significant precisely because it so actively resists simplification. Larkin writes, he says, in search of "the prolific in ordinary."[26] The apparent ordinariness is key, because these are also sacrifice zones, exemplifying the enduring hold the nature–culture binary has on the environmental imagination. Larkin shows how shadow places, unpeopled but not unpopulated, are distinctly lively, because the desires and consumption patterns of so many of us are *lived through* them. Excess is therefore a methodological principle, through which he returns again and again to a perception of the richness of what is ostensibly thin, depleted, or scarce.

Larkin writes in the late modernist tradition of the British Poetry Revival; more recently, Harriet Tarlo has aligned his work with a postwar movement of "radical landscape poetry."[27] He has called his idiosyncratic syntax an effort to "bring figurative clusters to some sort of edge or horizon."[28] The spatializing image here is significant, as Larkin's work shares an affinity with the notion of "composition by field" advocated in Charles Olson's projective verse. As Mandy Bloomfield has observed, open-field poetics visualize the artificiality of efforts to represent nonhuman lifeways, while at the same time performing the rich interrelations that exist between human and nonhuman.[29] In particular, by moving away from the set patterns of more regular, lyric forms, the distributive possibilities of open-field verse allow poets to explore entanglement as both a fact of being and a matter of ethics. Barad also asserts that diffraction is an "open field."[30] The opening stanza of "Five Plantation Clumps" can serve as an illustration of diffraction as a poetics:

> Somehow I can't help flocking to plantations of sallow inquest. As if obeyed that resentful pool made sheeny by perforated rest. A net, not fully woven onto narrow earth, of nearer, sparser horizons for anywhere shelterable yet. Five courses at an arc of tentative verve, a counter-furniture between preventable barren grain.[31]

The fully justified prose paragraph is a signature Larkin form. These great blocks of text recall the plantation's monocultural, monolithic presence in the landscape (Tsing's "uniform blocks"), and the hard edges and regular spacings of regimented lines suggest the infrastructure of managed stands, firebreaks, and access roads. But it is also, Larkin has noted, a means to highlight the nonscalable, "to allow all sorts of micro-cells and juxtapositions within the sentence-structure."[32] Internal rhymes and echoes suggest a more heterogeneous scene enfolded within the scalable blocks; the possible availability of "anywhere / shelterable yet." Enjambment also becomes significant, interrupting the seemingly impermeable block with intimations of a disruptive influence, highlighting the contingent ("as if / obeyed"; "net, not / fully woven") or oppositional ("counter- / furniture"). References to porosity also circulate throughout Larkin's poems, worrying away at the incomplete, the sparse, the networked, or the permeable. The effect is of a kind of coppiced verse, in which interrupting or cutting back the pathway of linear sense making in the poetic phrase or line stimulates the growth of other possible kinds of sense, new shoots that branch off in other directions. Although coppicing is not typically a feature of industrial conifer plantations of the kind Larkin visits, his "coppiced verse" gestures toward the long history of treating woods as a resource to be managed while also conjuring a sense of a fuller, more richly suggestive poem and place.

This approaches another key feature of Larkin's work, the impression of a kind of "hovering sense." His poems follow, broadly, a familiar syntax pattern but resist any final claim to sense-making. Rather, there is a sense of sympathetic but distinct components (perforated rest, narrow earth, sparser horizons) interleaved with one another. Barad says that diffraction does not fix in advance what is subject and what is object; rather, it allows us to examine the boundary-making practices that produce "subjects" and "objects," and other differences.[33] As if each element in the poem were passed through a diffraction grating, they arrange in phase, overlapping and intra-acting to amplify the richness of possibility in the scene.

As Jonathan Skinner has commented, "for Larkin, landscape is not so much a thing as a process, a kind of prosody marked by opening."[34] Landscapes, most particularly the industrial forest plantation, are "the terrain across which questions of technology and geopolitics arise."[35] "Across which" rather than "from where" or "out of which": as I will suggest, Larkin's poetics is informed by an attuned prepositional sensibility and alert to the relational possibilities made available in striated sites. "Site" involves a place "compounded of . . . jumps and oscillations. . . . How is a place stretched and folded, how is it ribbed and reinforced?"[36] Yet his focus revolves insistently around a landscape that might, conventionally, be called bounded. The plantation is for Larkin "a saturated object":[37]

overdetermined in terms of its value but also available to other kinds of rich commingling. Indeed, he finds particular value in their artificiality, which is to say their *scalability*:

> Given the element of the artificial, there is paradoxically an even sharper "edge" to these trees since such phalanxes come to an abrupt halt in places, are demarcation-riven, but that can be read by the poetry in a more negotiatory way, perhaps even offering a degree of un-innocent (because already harmed) redemption. We aren't wholly responsible for these trees, after all, and so how they respond in the poetry isn't simply what we might become in them.[38]

Here scalability leads, conversely, to a new understanding of relation. In particular, Larkin's modernist poetics acknowledge the existence of a networked world of interlaced organic and inorganic infrastructure; in Moore's terms, they allow us to "see resources as relational."[39]

Larkin's plantation investigations began in the 1990s and, as might be expected from such a persistent, forensic focus, have yielded a very precise vocabulary. Terms like *site, gift, relation,* and *horizon* are each freighted with a very finely calibrated ethics of place. Perhaps the most significant concept in Larkin's lexicon, though, is *scarce.* He traces the term's "strategic history," from an "index of demand" in the eighteenth century to what he calls "the concomitant of a theoretically infinite desire for consumption" in the twentieth, when "perennial scarcity" arose as "a relative and social dynamic"[40]—the dynamic of commodity frontiers such as shale gas and what Timothy Mitchell calls "carbon democracy."[41] Scarcity arises when nature is made scalable. In opposition to a logic of resource extraction, Larkin proposes a "scarcity of relation" grounded in the "givenness" of the world. Here *scarcity* describes a world whose "overflowingness" is real and available but also "fragile and scarce of access." Larkin's concept of scarcity therefore sets in motion a diffraction pattern, a kind of cut across the scalable.

Scarcity defines an irreducible way of being in the world, located in the unexpected, the uncanny, or the unruly: in other words, a way of being that is *nonscalable.* It is "a quality that is diminishable but rebounds in unexpected ways, not without distortion and loss but as gaining extension

and depth and new horizons of relations."[42] As with the matsutake mushroom, nonscalable relations expand the narrow horizons of the world
made scalable ("horizon," for Larkin, indicates that which opens out
onto relation). Scarcity's connection with the gift denotes "a mode of
finite being in which what needs to be given for human life to be at home
in the natural world has been given, but . . . not so as to constitute a sufficiency."[43] Larkin's scarcity maps a diffraction pattern, plotting "difference that goes alongside as well as cutting across."[44] As John Kinsella has
observed, his work engages with systems that are both "independent and
codependent."[45] Recalling Robert Frost's observation, "something there
is that does not love a wall," Larkin finds entropy a catalyst to relation.[46]
His "poetics of scarcity" is thus a passage to relation in the midst of a
smooth, simplified, scalable world.

The kinds of woodlands that appeal to Larkin are typically relatively
new growth, at times closer to scrub than forest (thickets, spinneys,
"miscellaneous clumps").[47] References to porosity circulate throughout
poems such as those collected in *Slights Agreeing Trees*: "Coupled or
cammed fluting, a porous belt stretches fenestration to / enmesh ovals
at canopy, beaches in wafer impenetrability."[48] While he stakes a claim
for "Horizon as pure gain above endlessness," we also find "the tree- /
clump tight-spaced, embodying horizon like a pigment of its frame";[49]
and in "Dur Hill," which commemorates a modern enclosure in the New
Forest, planted in the 1950s and 1960s, we learn that "Both access and
distance are plantable here, where they may not be, / in this greed grid,
interwoven, intervened, what they otherwise are / to each other."[50] In
Larkin's coppiced verse the play of light and the crowding of the field
summon a sense of the plantation as a site of negotiated needs and partially achieved vision:

> Tenuous pressing together. In a photo-herence slender returns on
> the openness of light: but unfelled radiance from this tender loss of
> result.[51]

The industrial forest is regulated and proscribed, but also consolidating
and illuminating; "photo-herence," in particular, calls to mind the optical

sense of coherence, which describes the arrangement of waves of light in phase. Contrary to the narrowing of vision that defines commercial forestry, Larkin's radiant plantations throw out light to the horizon. The perfection of optical coherence, however, is here uncertain: fragile, reduced, hedged. It is a "radiance embedded within insufficiency."[52] Thus, whereas Larkin can observe elsewhere that this "through-hallway is openly scant," it is "no / longer empty, but sent into sequels of reserve."[53] While "reserve" hails the shade of Martin Heidegger, Larkin has insisted that his work pursues a negotiation *with* rather than simply and directly opposing the enframing of organic abundance—it is interested less in the total reduction of nature to standing reserve than in the emergence of "a compacted and raked-over preserve, . . . which, despite the industrial handling, makes its returns magical and unprogressive."[54]

"Unprogressive" here signals Larkin's opposition to an accelerated and naturalized vision of infinite growth rather than a Luddite obduracy. He does not aspire to a restored purity of place or vision; whatever else the plantations might be or become in the poems, they are always *infrastructure,* and it is in rethinking our relations with this infrastructure, cultivating an art of noticing the dense arrangement of relations in ostensibly simplified environments, where we discover the principle that underpins his poetics of scarcity.

In this striving to achieve "the reversal of an inherited drift or disconnection,"[55] Larkin's work offers an Anthropocenic (or perhaps *plantationocenic*) form of what Terry Gifford has called "post-pastoral."[56] "A plantation," Larkin warns, "is not a garden feature, but a naturalised outdoor resource."[57] Consequently, while on occasion his work might offer a hint of lyrical grace notes—"an outyard of leafy arrows," "the dappled niche this side of it given"[58]—equally if not more often, other lexical registers shape the scene. In "Five Plantation Clumps," "fenestration," "embrasure," "embouchure," and "cristate" draw, variously, on architectonic, topographical, and botanical vocabulary to set up a diffraction pattern of overlaid associations that negotiate between openness and closure, the regular and the unruly ("keep the landscape's waxy / criblines stubby but cristate in the roads" suggests a knowing play on "crispate," which means to possess a wavy margin),[59] prospect and clump, limit and infinitude.

However, while he refuses to sugar the pill and propose to "redeem" a pastoral vision, Larkin nonetheless offers a forceful critique of, and alternative to, scalability. In "Plantations Parallels Apart," he observes that "Production rushes a spectre of world to sector, the human order / lacking spathe."[60] "Spathe" refers to the leaf or leaves that enclose a cluster of flowers; thus the semiotics of organic growth are rudely excluded by the improvident rush to reduce "world to sector."

Larkin's plantations, by contrast, are what Tsing calls "polyphonic assemblages":

> Mechanised forest for its contribution intensity, its blinding input, the spatial-cornered as world, but as idyll crannied and packed, unable to be sole picking of its industrial-forestial origin. Put purity through this cable and proliferate the convergent riddle, the divergent middle of bind.[61]

For Tsing, the notion of the assemblage opens up a prospect of "world-making projects, human and non-human" within commodified landscapes;[62] similarly, for Larkin, the plantation's "block of / green, ... sprained of recovery" also conveys a "green sharpness."[63] According to Robert Baird, an important element of Larkin's poetics is his use of the "antipun," neologisms or epentheses that "make familiar words stranger, as one connotation drives another (usually the more obvious) into hiding."[64] Thus "unicited green" conveys a sense of converging lifeways within the monocultural framework, suggesting both singularity of place and reference ("uni-cited" / "uni-sited") and commingling ("united").[65] "Know a plantation," he writes, "by what it does up / to plurals."[66] We might say that Larkin's sometimes tenuous or spiky lines are a response to what Tsing calls "the pixelated quality of the expansion-oriented world."[67]

As infrastructure, Larkin's plantations are inherently relational sites. That is, they instantiate the complex of salvage projects and multispecies world-making from which the particular lifeway of the twenty-first-century Western human subject emerges, as well as the insistent drive to simplify that obscures this density of entanglements. Plantations therefore offer a rather precarious form of shelter; yet, as Tsing observes, "precarity *is* the condition of our time. . . . What we imagine as trivial [is] the centre of

the systematicity we seek."[68] It is in this diffractive sense of the entanglement of an individual lifeway in numerous other lifeways that Larkin's
poetics of scarcity reaches into deep time. As Barad states, "diffractions
are untimely," dissolving the notion of an absolute boundary "between
here-now and there-then."[69] Thus we have that

> A detonation of striped, reclothed light is no horizon to be offered at
> empty sight, more a deferred relic of future limit, distances which cannot
> lie open but which must be prematurely sown. This is the offer covering
> forwards, slight sites of it don't grow further toward. Fettered by intimacy,
> lesser in place to be a cell like distance, and mark of the fore-spoil of true
> preliminary spindles on behalf of. Green refreshment at its slackening net
> emitting the arrest.[70]

This is a particularly "untimely" passage. Just as light diffracts through
the gaps between tree and leaf, as anterior and posterior gestures in the
poem interleave, they conjure a sense of simultaneity; as a "deferred relic
of future limit," the plantation becomes a site of temporal intra-action,
marked by long pasts of human management ("environing," as hinted at in
"fettered by intimacy" and "arrest," and the dual meanings of "cell") and
anticipated futures that cannot admit unchecked growth. This anticipated
future reconditions our understanding of the past of appropriation and
salvage that the plantation memorializes, reinforced by Larkin's prepositional sensibility, as "toward," "at," "on behalf of" introduce a sense of
contingent relations (or scarcity of relation).

Larkin's poems reintroduce a sense of time to sites captured by scalability. Making scalable means uprooting both literally and figuratively,
cutting the connections that Kohn says constitute the thought life of
the forest and muting its entangled semiotics. The only time available
to the plantation, according to the logic that forms it, is that of the commodity form. Yet Tsing also shows how these sites contain multiple
other temporalities. "All natural history," she writes, "is a history of
disturbance."[71] Disturbance is the dynamic principle behind ecological
diversity, an inevitable and continual aspect of all ecosystems (whether
supposedly "pristine" or "damaged"). In particular, disturbance is evident
in what Tsing calls "blasted landscapes," the ruins of industrial sites (or

"post-plantations") that provide the conditions for collaborative organisms, such as the matsutake mushroom, to thrive. Matsutake forests depend on "certain historical trajectories": a bare mineral soil, stripped of organic nutrients by burning; specialized flora, such as pine trees; and *time,* at least thirty or forty years, which is roughly how long it takes for mushrooms to appear. In this time, matsutake create multiple, smaller disturbances, blocking the cycling of organic matter so that a buildup of humus does not lessen the dominance of the pioneer species on which they depend.[72] Thus, as she says, "disturbance realigns possibilities for transformative encounter": rather than Uexküll's "bubble worlds," Tsing advocates studying the "shifting cascades of collaboration and complexity," where "many histories come together."[73]

Disturbance therefore emerges in Tsing's work as a way to rethink relations in time, and who and what and where can be said to possess a history. Tsing's efforts to historicize multispecies collaboration "draw evolution back into history." "History," she affirms, "plays havoc with scalability."[74] Larkin's work, similarly, examines the teeming possibilities and temporalities that inhabit what he calls the "thrive-margin."[75] In "Hollow Woods Allow," from 2013, Larkin visits Mear's Plantation in Gloucestershire, where a worked-out limestone quarry "forms an under-bowl to woodland . . . an outline of attenuation and vertical counterstrikes." The limestone is conducive to both ash and beech trees ("though not dense," he qualifies) and to a rich understory including old man's beard, hart's-tongue, woodruff, and shadow-stinted bramble.[76] The emphasized sparseness is picked up throughout, both in the poem's open-field arrangement and by association, and thereby revised, so as "not to outgrow a gap but sieve it otherwise," with an eye towards an unsettling of "slender means."[77] In particular, Larkin revises the sense of "hollow" as depletion, to signify hollow as aperture: the "hollowed out" site ("empty of stone") becomes a passage or opening on to relation, as in "a bowl out of its prior scarcity rehung to a / differently given-out."[78] Typographically, the intermittent use of expanded spacings can be read as minor disturbances.

Furthermore, on each page of "Hollow Trees Allow," Larkin's more characteristic prose blocks bookend a clutch of between two and four more slender stanzas, of varying length but typically two or three beat lines, set in a broad expanse of white space. The insets aren't fully justified in the manner of Larkin's prose paragraphs and appear to the eye as a form of more conventional lyric presence (another kind of disturbance, perhaps, of Larkin's modernist field), although they are equally resistant to sense-making. This prosimetrum effect further accentuates the sense of a site (and a poem) that contains the possibility of relation:

> a monostorm of absence
> caught at a culled void
> multiple templates of minute
> accent finding next
> lignins of trust[79]

Lignin is an organic polymer deposited in the cell walls of vascular plants, providing rigidity and structure and conducting water through the plant body. Lignin is also, after cellulose, the most plentiful source of renewable carbon and, because of its slow rate of decomposition, a significant component of the humus that can build up in postindustrial sites where the soil has been depleted, creating advantageous conditions for the understory to thrive. Following the "monostorm of absence," "lignins of trust" accumulate as the new plantation gathers together and diversifies its "ecology of selves." Mear's Plantation is therefore a site in which, as Tsing proposes, "humans join others in making landscapes of unintentional design."[80]

The colonization of Mear's Plantation by ash and beech demonstrates how something of the semiotic breadth Kohn attributes to tropical forests can emerge through disturbance in former industrial sites. As Tsing explains, pines are a particularly good illustration of the collaborative history of seemingly blasted sites. Modern pine forests exemplify the dehistoricizing process of scalability. Pines are planted "as a potentially constant and unchanging resource"; the goal, according to Tsing, is to "remove pines from indeterminate encounters, and thus their ability to make history"[81]—to isolate them from anything that would contaminate their value. Nonetheless, as a classic pioneer species, pines are "among the most active trees on earth," ideally adapted to "open and disturbed landscapes." They exemplify how multispecies histories come together:

Pines live in extreme environments because of the help they get from mycorrhizal fungi. Fossils have been found from fifty million years ago that show root associations between pines and fungi. . . . Even the anatomy of pine roots has been formed in association with fungi. Pines put out "short roots," which become the site of mycorrhizal association. If no fungi encounter them, the short roots abort. (In contrast, fungi do not cover at least the tips of anatomically different "long roots," specialized for exploration.) By moving across disturbed landscapes, pines make history, but only through their association with mycorrhizal companions.[82]

Although Larkin does not engage with fungi as Tsing does, in his explorations of disturbed landscapes, his encounters with pines describe a similar sense of a repudiated collaborative history—that history denied in the arrangement of shadow places.

In "Turf Hill," from *Slights Agreeing Trees,* Larkin encounters a sacrifice zone marked by a rich entanglement of infrastructures. Turf Hill (as he explains in a topographical note) is a "much reduced" plantation in the New Forest, pierced by an east–west line of electricity pylons:[83]

Some livery to simplify a real shank through the wards, power-lines at a slope of conduction with rapid incomplete owing of ground. To blow with spreading on the grid some green flutter of smaller rigid body.

Not covert and long not to be covered in links of shadow, a joined way lifts itself into fringe. The pylon avenue isn't corridor pulse interceding with plantation, but ventilation as if by air-arc of the horizons within clump. To displenish beside refreshed ground, what is healed and hugs shaft but never swings anew upon line-break. Grit at the big branch, anti-tentacular of hung community, but generously ferned.

How the boles thin to the widener of tracking turf, pylon by terrace of heeded instrument! If the tree-standing for wire is the pull of cantileaf, what can indent its continuous ornament looping on power-line? The trees are resident by unavailing advantage, full technical sorrow lattices their derivative store of staying beside-hand a cloaked way below. Each wafer strut an actuator, soft spring between wing and store. Field follower across overhead pitch, into the straits which fertilise a neb of impasse, but where wire cups to its beak a lift of towers inciting local spine, so spike your green along. Forked untransformable at heel of branch, trees topped for their sail-at-root, they bare these iron masts whenever nothing can have happened to the great limb.[84]

In contrast with Heaney's driving poems, here Larkin foregrounds the materiality of infrastructure. Terms associated with electrical infrastructure (pulse, cable, conduction, flashover, actuator, wards, wire, circuitry, insulation, output) proliferate, in combination with arboreal phrases (bole, clump, heel of branch); in particular, conjunctive words and phrases ("links," "power-lines," and "line-breaks"; "forked," "latticed") suggest Larkin's interest in tensile relations. The poem presents us with trees and pylons—and, by implication, vastly different temporal and spatial scales—*in phase*. Tree and pylon fold and unfold in a kind of superposition: "full technical sorrow lattices" the trees' "derivative store"; "Each wafer strut as actuator, soft spring between wing and store"; and later, "Incompressible flow knows the studded circuitry of tree load."[85] The poem thus acts as a kind of diffraction apparatus, an aperture through which we can, in Barad's words, "attend . . . to the relational nature of difference"[86]—in this sense, the differences that attend ostensibly simplified commodities. Larkin pursues a complex enclosure, not simply a conspicuous striation: the effect of the pylon avenue is not to intercede—to intervene from without—but rather a kind of "ventilation" contiguous with the horizon (i.e., the possibility of opening out into relation) *within* the cluster of trees. "Cantileaf," another "antipun," makes this explicit, connoting a sense of balanced torsions ("cantileaver") and through this the inter-*leaving* of pines and pylons that, collaboratively, mark the site both as standing reserve and as something more—a site of relational scarcity, where relations become visible in their entanglement.

In "Turf Hill," Larkin provides a frame through which to see the plantation in its plurality. His diffractive attention brings to mind both the pylons' *and* the trees' place as scalable entities. This conjunction calls to mind Naomi Klein's observation that "power from fossil fuels always required sacrifice zones," neglected or disenfranchised areas deemed expendable before the needs of the carbon age, whether in "the black lungs of coal miners" or in indigenous communities evicted from their forest homes that have been set aside as carbon sinks.[87] Not only this, however, as Larkin places scalable entities *in unruly relation,* thereby inviting readers not only to think across the multiple scales of energy production and consumption, and the costs involved but also to think more carefully about what Etienne Benson calls the "lively environments" in which all scalable infrastructure is situated.[88] Benson has traced how "envirotechnical" solutions were devised by U.S. engineers in the 1920s to mask the fact that infrastructures also have environments. Just as pine plantations were designed to isolate pines from disruptive encounters, as Tsing describes, successive redesigns of the electrical system sought to create a buffer between infrastructure and environment. In particular, Benson cites the problem of electrical flashovers—arcs of current that create short-circuits by leaping from the wires to the towers—caused by the excrement of birds perched on the transmission towers. The birds' "streamers" were an unwelcome reminder of the unruliness of the environment surrounding the grid. The solution was to install forms of "bioinsulation": pans to catch the excrement and spikes to prevent perching.[89] In each case, Larkin's poem tacitly invokes and reframes these efforts to insulate *against* life. "So spike your green along," by employing the verb form, reappraises this as a dynamic, not an inert, system; the lines "flashovers of insulation are stroked / transversely by the branches' own shield cable" gesture to the way electricity resists capture as inventory.[90]

As Benson says, "electricity is not a thing, but rather an unruly process that can only be turned to human ends with great effort and then only partially."[91] Rather than fixed and passive structures, then, as Bennett has argued, electrical infrastructure constitutes an assemblage, including not just "humans and their constructions" but also "some very active and powerful nonhumans: electrons, trees, wind, electromagnetic fields."[92] Larkin's poem reminds us that, contrary to their appearance, neither the power lines nor the plantation is inert; rather, both are caught up in larger processes of intra-active semiotics: decomposed Carboniferous plant life is extracted and converted to energy by human–machinic assemblages and must then be insulated against the creeping influence of the later forest environment it pulses through; birds find perches on the transmission towers that resemble branches, then humans design modifications to dissuade or negate the negative effects (streamers) of this appropriation, all entangled in a lively, human–avian–arboreal–electrical collaboration in world-making.

Barad notes that, if our goal is to think the social and the natural together, we need a method that does so "without defining the one against the other and holding either as the fixed referent for understanding the other. What are needed," she says, "are diffraction apparatus to study these entanglements."[93] Larkin's revision of the apparently thin and inert scene of Turf Hill presents a site thickened with relations, unpeopled but crucially not unpopulated, providing a framework for thinking of the entanglement of pylon and plantation as mutually transformative entities, weaving together deep and shallow time, organic and inorganic. Larkin's poetics of scarcity remakes the plantation as "an imposition which still retains an opportunity of becoming more slight, more self-attentive,"[94] and it is through this reframed attention to the irrepressible relationality of life, in the face of the hegemony of the scalable, that a fuller realization of what he calls "selvages of field" becomes possible.[95] His work proposes that within the salvage operations that relentlessly seek to simplify the world into inventory or waste, ecologies of selves can persist and even thrive: not in the plenitude of sufficiency but in relations of scarcity that are open to but do not presume upon the givenness of the world.

EVELYN REILLY: PLASTIC PLENITUDE

Anna Tsing is not alone in thinking the future is mushroom shaped. In 2014, *The Future of Plastic,* an exhibition commissioned by Fondazione PLART in Napoli, included an innovative project to use mushrooms to mimic the properties of plastic. Maurizio Montalti of design studio Officina Corpuscoli and Hans Wösten, a microbiologist at Utrecht University, developed a technique to transform fungal mycelium into a new plastic-resembling material. Mycelium is a gluelike substance composed of the network of threadlike filaments, or hyphae, through which nutrients are transmitted between fungi and tree roots. In other words, it is the conduit for transformative mutualism. Hyphae possess many of the same features as common thermoplastics—elasticity, a high strength-to-weight ratio, homogeneity, and hydrophobicity (water repelling)—and Montalti and

Wösten have since curated a range of new products that use "mycelium design." For instance, fungal polyominoes are a building material that exploits mycelium's capacity to form strong bonds with other organic materials; Fungi Mutarium is a project seeking to grow edible fungi on plastic waste.[96] Their intention is to highlight the need to find organic replacements for the oil-intensive and supply-chain-dependent processes that produce plastic (and plastic waste, including the approximately 8 million metric tons dumped in the world's oceans each year).

Mycelium design presents "a critical vision of plastics," in the words of Marco Petroni, curator of *The Future of Plastic*.[97] Others, however, have expressed doubts. Writing in *New Scientist*, Sjef van Gaalen suggested that mycelium's utilitarian benefits might not be enough to resolve consumers' aesthetic reservations. As more fungal products appear (packaging, insulation), van Gaalen predicts they will do so slowly and "unseen until their fruiting bodies break ground."[98] For now, plastic's supremacy is assured.

Plastic is a miraculous substance. We mold it into the shape of our desires. Plastic can emit or absorb light; be rigid or ductile, immensely strong but light; insulate, protect, or seal. Yet to grasp almost any plastic object is almost certainly to be presented with a very particular and limited set of shared characteristics: smoothness, fluency, and invisibility. Each key on the keyboard on which I type has a slight concavity to better accommodate my fingertips. The plastic bottle I drink from has also been shaped to sit easily in my hand, with a ridged cap that twists off with minimal pressure. I take medication each day that is vacuum packed to prevent contamination (of the medicine, and therefore of me). Each material recedes into the background of my experience, tacitly discouraging me from noticing the work it does facilitating my interaction with the world.

Plastic is a form of realism. It gives the world to us as we, in the West, have been taught to see it: pliable, frictionless, immediately available, and smoothed to our advantage. Its synthetic origins situate it in a world of pervasive unseeing; we are trained to look past the multiple ways in which plastics intervene in daily life. It is, as Roland Barthes put it, "ubiquity made visible," less a thing in itself than a trace of the many actions and movements it makes possible.[99] Designed to fall away from vision as soon as its use value has been exhausted, plastic, Jeffrey Meikle says, "has been naturalized."[100] It is the ultimate scalable material, presenting consumers with the utopia of uniformity, of endless replicable experiences; it distills the world into a series of frictionless surfaces and tessellating shapes.

Plastic is therefore a deeply ideological material, as much as the fossil fuels we burn to contract time and space to the orbit of our longings. And similarly, plastic has significantly conditioned how consumer societies in particular appreciate and experience time. This is due not only to the way plastics reduce friction but also to the fantasy of disposability they promise. The assurance that it will disappear when its usefulness is exhausted or suspended is implicit in almost any plastic object. Bernadette Bensaude-Vincent writes that plastics "invite us to experience the instant for itself as detached from the flux of time."[101] Timelessness is therefore a key element of what Bensaude-Vincent calls plastic's utopian dimension, the dream of dematerialization.[102] This timeless smoothness is, of course, just a dream. Plastic may appear to be a utopian material—ushering our smooth passage through a trace world of desires, divorced from the material world—but it nonetheless possesses both a dynamic and complex historicity and a deeply entangled and intra-active capability.

Plastics are "unruly technologies"—that is, they do not conform to the well-disciplined states we expect of them.[103] Plasticizers, substances added to enhance the flexibility of thermoplastics, are not inextricably bound to the polymer chains they bond with and can be broken. They also mimic hormones and can therefore create unwanted changes in the bodies of living creatures. Off-gassing from the flame-retardant polybromiated diphenyl ether (PBDE) in my keyboard and the chair I'm sitting in, and phthalates in my office carpet, mean that the ostensibly frictionless environment in which I write is in fact vibrant with endocrine-disrupting chemicals, leaching from the plastics around me into my body. The polystyrene in my bike helmet is also an endocrine disruptor, and if I chose to take the bus to work instead of cycling, the thermal paper on which my ticket is printed may contain bisphenol A (BSA). Each of these chemicals has its origins in the alignment of military and industrial capital. Polystyrene was developed by Union Carbide, the U.S. chemical giant responsible for the 1984 Bhopal disaster; polyethylene terephthalate (PET, commonly used to package bottled water) was devised by DuPont in the 1940s, a company that supplied 40 percent of Allied gunpowder in the First World War and also developed Freon, the chlorofluorocarbon linked to ozone depletion. Plastic connects each of us to these violent histories. As Adam Dickinson observes, "my body wears industrial, agricultural, and military history whether I like it or not."[104]

Just as Tsing advocates the need to tell the history of the pine tree, to fully embrace plastic's lively entanglements, as well as define a poetics of sacrifice zones, we need to apprehend the temporal complexity that underpins its apparent smoothness. These histories operate across vastly different scales. Drawing on A. N. Whitehead's observation that molecules must be understood as "historical rather than physical" entities,[105] Bensaude-Vincent and Isabelle Stengers call plastic an "informed material," which becomes richer in information through polymerization.[106] It is also bound up with often damaging "pre-" and "afterlives" of resource extraction and disposal. The sixty-day life-span of a single-use plastic container is informed not only by the various industrial and chemical processes (often working with materials violently extracted from shadow places) that shape it but by the vast, deep pasts and futures it also embodies: by the millions of years it took for the raw materials (oil) to form and the ten thousand years it will take for the plastic to break down.[107] As Anthony Andrady has observed, the processes of degradation and mineralization in plastics are so slow that it is reasonable to suppose that all common plastics ever produced that were not incinerated remain present in the environment.[108] While plastic encourages us to inhabit a series of detached moments, then, it also inducts us into a deeply strange and complex entanglement of time scales and processes, as deep pasts and futures hedge each fleeting moment of consumption.

Plastic's utopian properties, its scalability, and its capacity to disappear behind the vision of order and smoothness it projects conceal the fact that it is a deeply intra-active substance. Plastic *is* the environment many of us live in; as Jody Roberts makes plain, for some, it makes life possible.[109] To be "in the open," then, is to be surrounded by plastic. Not only this, but the mutability of plastic, originally a characteristic of human invention ("plasticity" as a feature of the creative mind), "enables particular sorts of humans to emerge."[110] Plastics are the surfaces on which the posthuman subject is inscribed. Plastic drainage pipes, fiber-optic cables, replacement heart valves, smartphone screens, and multiple more banal objects from carrier bags and shrink-wrapping to the BIC pen all collaborate to produce "the human" in the twenty-first century. It is almost certain that you have plastic somewhere on your person as you read this—as buttons, spectacle frames, or the aglets on your shoelaces (as well as *in* your person, given the quantities of marine plastic debris that have entered the food chain). To appreciate the timeliness of plastic, we need to think of it as what Serenella Iovino and Serpil Oppermann call "storied matter," through which capitalist structures and unruly molecules weave a trace world of desires and material relations.[111]

Evelyn Reilly's *Styrofoam* explores the complex and entangled, relational material behind the smooth and scalable experience of plastic. Influences as diverse as Ezra Pound, Gertrude Stein, Elaine Scarry, St. Teresa of Avila, Wikipedia, *The Divine Comedy,* and the work of neurologist Vittorio Gallese circulate, congeal, and break apart in emulation of the sumps of plastic particulates that form the five Pacific and Atlantic garbage patches. Added to this is an eclectic mix of registers, from lyrical and scientific voices to advertising copy, video games, and horror films, and set alongside the various grammars of the visual and plastic arts—photography, painting, sculpture, scientific diagrams—distributed throughout the text. Reilly's affinities with Language and post-Language poetry and interest in the interconnectedness of semiotic systems produces a particularly plastic verse through collage, cultural cross-reference, and an Olsonian spaciousness.[112] But *Styrofoam* explores how, behind the bounded orbit of plastic's apparent "thingness" ("the promise," as Heather Davis says, "of sealed, perfected, clean, smooth abundance"), there lies a more volatile, unstable materiality.[113] To treat a plastic object as the thing itself entails also the vast, transformative processes it takes part in—the traces of movement that conjure the dream of modernity. As with Larkin, what emerges is a kind of diffractive poetics that gives form to the dense, pliant weave of relations that make and remake perceptions of the plasticized world.

The collection's ostensibly very direct title also immediately introduces an ambiguity: Styrofoam, a trademarked form of closed-cell extruded polystyrene foam typically used in thermal insulation and as a crafting material, is often used colloquially (and incorrectly) in North America to refer to the *expanded* polystyrene foam used to make everyday objects like disposable cups and packaging material. By positioning her investigation at this boundary between the commodified and colloquial linguistic registers, Reilly highlights capitalism's role in shaping how we use language and thus our responses to the world around us. The ambiguity admits an array of other thermoplastics, a subset of pliable materials that soften and solidify at particular temperatures. Thermoplastics exemplify the ontology of plastics—what Barthes calls "the very idea of its infinite transformation."[114] Whereas thermosetting polymers form indissoluble bonds, thermoplastics do not fully crystalize (retaining a degree of irregularity or entanglement in their structure) and thus preserve a degree of malleability. Because crystals act in a manner similar to a diffraction grate, crystallization (and thus plasticity) is measured by X-ray diffraction; to put it another way, it is by diffraction that we can observe plasticity.

Both its materiality and its ontology declare plastic a deeply intraactive substance. To tell the stories of plastic—to fully appreciate it as a "relational resource" rather than a "utopian material"[115]—we need therefore to think about plastic in terms of the relational becoming of intra-action, or, as Gabrys, Hawkins, and Michael put it, the "emergent and contingent" within the material.[116]

In *Styrofoam,* Reilly develops an "anti-pure" poetics that gives form to the entangled materiality and ontology of plastic: plastic appears less a substance than a principle of intra-action.[117] Her poetics embraces the malleability of thermoplastics. Punctuation is a key feature: open parentheses ("amid immortality of plastic (the ex- / of exhilaration (the ex- / of anonymity") signify an inclusive sensibility, as do Reilly's frequent plays on prefixes and suffixes.[118] The formative prefix "Ex-", indicating a sending out, is picked up throughout *Styrofoam* in both the problematized transcendence of Bernini's *Ecstasy of St Theresa* (a major node in "Wing/ Span/Screw/Cluster (Aves)") and in the frequent allusions to extinction.

By contrast, the superlative adjectival suffix -*est* (from the Middle English *este,* signifying consent, grace, bountifulness, or harmony) in "The Whiteness of Foam" introduces a gift sensibility that sets the totalizing (whiteout) effect of plastic against the nontotalizable relationality of the gift.

Lynn Keller notes that Reilly's "digitally inflected punctuation" frequently recalls the language of internet domain names and coding to explore multiple ways of forming connections in language.[119] As J. Hillis Miller has observed in a reflection on the poetics of cyberspace, such assemblages invoke the milieu of relentless solicitations we receive from technologized capitalist society. Poetic spacing in this context "is not innocent."[120] MacKenzie Wark has described how codework texts, which frame an antagonistic dialogue between different kinds of written communication, propose "new kinds of sense making" in the midst of "a chaotic space of temporary orders constantly becoming randomised."[121] The linkages implied by Reilly's punctuation suggest the depth of intraactive world-making processes in which plastic is involved. The poems convey a nuanced, *antagonistic* sense of plastics' relationality through her restless, inventive use of collage and typography. In Reilly's anarchic plastic world, plastic emerges as a densely storied material constituted by a thickly entangled meshwork of relations, histories, and times.

Reilly's poetics works with abundance and excess. "A Key to the Family of Thermoplastics" provides a new taxonomy, a kind of reimagining of the resin identification code, celebrating the profusion of plastics in everyday life. But the banal materialities gradually morph into a series of structural, biopolitical, and military–industrial forms of violence. Reilly's diffractive arrangement exposes the intimate relation between contexts of banality and violence. For instance, PTE migrates from its origin in the refinement of uranium to manufacture the atomic bombs dropped on Hiroshima and Nagasaki to a range of everyday uses and domestic contexts. The poem offers a kind of deranged catalog, revealing the hidden histories masked by plastics' utopian appearance, through which plastic emerges reenvisaged as the emanation of undead histories of violence, a kind of "ZOMBIE CORNUCOPIA."[122] It ends with dialogue excerpted from John Carpenter's *The Thing* (1962) and Irvin Yeaworth's *The Blob*

(1958), ironically calling into question the implications of "UNCON-TROLLED GROWTH."[123]

Like Larkin's plantations, plastic emerges in *Styrofoam* as a series of open fields—molecular, cultural, and topographical. A vibrant relationality is therefore encoded in the form of Reilly's poems. She assembles a "polymerized" poetics in which chains of association continually form, degrade, and re-form. Polymers are long chains of molecules that arrange in irregular and entangled formations when heated and can therefore be reshaped. *Styrofoam* consists of multiple short chains that resemble oligomers, molecular complexes of limited chains of monomers that combine to form long chains in the production of synthetic polymers. Thus the short-chain clusters in Reilly's poems, such as "Chlorophyll . daffodil . poly-fill," from "Daffodil.Gondola.Polystyrene" (a poem filled with allusions to Byron and Wordsworth), combine to shape an inquisitive, nonteleological approach. According to the polymerized logic of Reilly's poems, in which multiple recombinations are possible ("capable of being deformed continuously without rupture"),[124] the short chains shape a more distributed set of associations. "What the sea brought: poly.flotsam. faux.foam // &Floam®," from "Hence Mystical Cosmetic over Sunset Landfill" (another Melville reference), suggests more of a tidalectic motion.[125] Floam, a crafting material made from a mix of clay and polystyrene microbeads, is picked up later in the poem in the reference to phloem, the tissue in vascular plants that carries the nutrients produced during photosynthesis. This collocation of synthetic and botanical homophones queries what count as aberrations in a plasticized world. World-making and -unmaking emerge in the poem as continuous, open-ended processes; as an unnamed interlocutor observes, "It's not necessarily the end of the world, / just of this particular one."[126] Reilly's polymerized poetry brings into the open the entanglement and irregularity beneath thermoplastics' smooth surfaces. "All this.formation / anddeformation" counters the narrative of plastic as an inert material.[127]

Whereas Larkin frequently uses monolithic stanza forms to explore the diversity embedded within the simplified, Reilly's malleable approach to allusion, collage, punctuation, and genre pursues a more open, collocational use of space:

the opposite of snow   but of like white

the poly.mere.est.echt.thermoplastic

which becomes soft and malleable when heated
without change in its intrinsic properties

molded   whiteuponwhite   whitestwhiteness   –est –est[128]

In contrast with Larkin's condensed, saturated prose stanzas, in this extract
from "The Whiteness of Foam," Reilly explores the relational possibilities
available in open space to provoke a more pliable appreciation of plastic as
vibrant matter. Its superlative whiteness, which for Melville is the origin of
the "panic to the soul" provoked by the whale's "ghastly whiteness,"[129] is
the source of an uncanny transitivity. Styrofoam invites us to think again
about the associations that whiteness brings: not innocence, cleanliness,
or absence but a teeming, leaky, permeable, and therefore *ironic* set of
associations. The irony of "to ride on the heat of y/our own melting," set
against an Arctic backdrop, is in keeping with a recurring emphasis on the
hazardous liveliness plastic introduces to the environment.[130]

    Styrofoam began, Reilly says, as a "celebration of human creative
plasticity, but quickly engaged ironies such as aesthetic versus environmental notions of 'the eternal.'"[131] Creativity and the plastic arts remain
a preoccupation in *Styrofoam,* from the uses of plastic in craft activities
to the Romantics' reflections on imaginative and linguistic plasticity.
However, as the opening lines of the collection indicate, Reilly's abiding
concern is time, particularly the very deep time of seemingly inert but in
fact very lively substances:

    Answer: Styrofoam deathlessness.
    Question: How long does it take?[132]

The inverted question form signifies a nagging, persistent anxiety regarding
the apparent "deathlessness" of plastic. Heather Davis has observed that
plastic is particularly valued for its "quality of the undead," its capacity
to seal off and preserve.[133] If, as Tom Fisher puts it, everyday plastics are

"part of our 'extended self' . . . us extended into objects,"[134] a portion of this anxiety stems from the sense that this deathlessness is coincident with the projection of a contemporary human presence into the very deep future. The haunting augury of Styrofoam's ostensible deathlessness disorients linear perspectives on time: it is the distant future here, now, in plastic form.

It is an abiding irony in *Styrofoam* that the dynamism Reilly finds in thermoplastics seems at odds with the ecological sterility they contribute to, admitting "*not* (even) *the cheerful greenness of complete decay*" (another borrowing from Melville)[135] — that its apparent "deathlessness" is linked to so much death. "Permeable Mutual Design," a riff on the proliferation of polyethylene (the most commonly used form of plastic, including in the shampoo and toilet cleaner bottles Jamie discovers on Ceann Ear), is followed by a pair of images: Rudolph Stingel's *Untitled* (2000), for which the artist walked across four Styrofoam panels in boots laced with a chemical astringent, embedding his footprints in the surface, and the haunting image of a set of polar bear tracks in a white snowfield, titled *Ursus Anonymous* (2008). Reilly has described how the poems were inspired by viewing Stingel's Styrofoam sculptures at the Whitney Museum of American Art. The pairing of two sets of trace presence in very different materials invites viewers to consider what are the lively points of intra-action whereby each receives the impression of the other. As Gabrys, Hawkins, and Michael put it, "plastics set in motion relations between things that become sites of responsibility and effect."[136] Recall Jamie's assertion that "the breast milk of polar bears has chemicals in it";[137] studies have shown that xenoendocrine pollutants, including plastics, have reduced reproduction among East Greenland and Svalbard polar bears.[138] Plastic is thus collaborating in the production of a more precarious world for the polar bear, remaking the physiology of the bear itself even as it strides toward death. The counterpointing of Stingel's *Untitled* with *Ursus Anonymous* crosses Reilly's challenge to the perceived sterility and inertia of plastic with a future haunted by the loss of biodiversity.

As already noted, *Styrofoam*'s liveliness is in part due to the richness of its intertexts (as we shall see, intertextuality is also a key element in the poetics of kin-making described in the next chapter). These other references are largely fragments, often degraded in some way and worked into the fabric of Reilly's polymerized text. Principal among this polyvocal "poly.flotsam" are Melville's "The Whiteness of the Whale," D. H. Lawrence's "The Ship of Death," and Samuel Taylor Coleridge's "The Rime of the Ancient Mariner."[139] The interplay between the three, and their shared concern with the treatment of the sea as resource or shadow place, means that they form another kind of short chain of associations through which multiple echoes—of risk, pollution, and ecological damage—sound.

"The Whiteness of Foam," invokes the *Dawn Princess,* a cruise ship involved in a fatal collision in Glacier Bay, Alaska, in 2001, with a pregnant humpbacked whale (identified by a marine survey in 1975 and nicknamed "Snow" by researchers for the white markings on her flukes in a further, buried reference to Melville). Reilly reconfigures the cruise ship as the "little ark" from Lawrence's poem: "Oh build your ship of death, your little ark."[140] Irony is heaped upon irony; the 77,441-metric-ton *Dawn Princess* is reconceived as an ark that brings animal death rather than conserving life; in contrast with Ahab's murderous pursuit, Snow is killed accidentally, a consequence of our deadly disregard for other species. Lawrence's poem is a kind of existential threnody figured as pastoral collapse; in *Styrofoam,* it is the appropriation of cheap nature that determines the shift from green plenitude into sterile whiteness, a studied unseeing that has lethal consequences.

The problem of unseeing is not limited to the exploitation of marine resources. It is estimated that the world's seas contain between 100 and 150 million metric tons of plastic debris, concentrated in five enormous gyres in the Pacific and Atlantic oceans. The majority of the waste comes from commercial fishing, discarded packaging, and naval or commercial vessels.[141] Large plastic objects that enter the oceans break up into plastic particulates only millimeters in diameter, weakened by exposure to UV light and the harrying of waves; alternatively, they enter the oceans as microfibers rinsed from synthetic clothing by washing machines or as microbeads, the raw material of a huge array of different consumer goods (particularly cosmetics). These microplastics are easily dispersed, being lighter than water, and, once picked up by ocean currents, can travel vast distances (there are reported incidents of plastic waste from Japan arriving on Midway Atoll, four thousand kilometers to the east).[142] Recent estimates suggest the oceans contain up to 5 trillion individual pieces of plastic particulate, some of which has been found at depths of more than three thousand meters in concentrations one thousand times greater than at the surface.[143] Much of this plastic waste carries endocrine-disrupting chemicals, such as polychlorinated biphenyl, organochlorine pesticides, flame retardants, and petroleum hydrocarbons. Far from the desert of inert, "deathless" waste, this "plastic soup" is, as Jennifer Gabrys has observed, "a site of continual metamorphosis and intra-actions."[144] The oceans are home to an estimated one thousand microorganisms that have evolved to colonize plastic debris (often polystyrene),[145] and many ocean plastics have absorptive properties, accumulating in toxic sinks that pass high concentrations of dangerous chemicals into the food chain.

The "deathlessness" of plastic that is queering the world's oceans is underscored by its vibrancy; the volatility of many thermoplastics means that they enter a "dying" state almost from the point of molding (hence Fisher notes that the "new" smell given off by PVC "comes from the volatile elements of the material evaporating from it; a key result of this volatility is the death of the material as it becomes less 'plastic'").[146] As these elements include endocrine-disrupting phthalates, it becomes clear that liveliness and deathlessness are entangled in complex arrangements in the life of plastic. We can perhaps understand the "death drive" of "undead" plastic as, to borrow from Slavoj Žižek's reading of Freud, "an uncanny *excess* of life."[147]

This is evident in the first poem in the collection, "Hence Mystical . . . ," which troubles the linear story of extraction, consumption, and disposal. Reilly's inversion is true to the "immanence" of waste that Gay Hawkins identifies in all economic transactions: the logic of disposability means that plastic does not become waste but is *always already* waste even as the raw materials are drawn from the strata.[148] Reilly's poem, which contemplates a landfill site, is a song of waste that invites reflection on the uncanny entanglements and time scales of plastic pollution. As Myra

Hird has observed, waste is not inert or static; rather, "waste flows." Whether buried in landfill or washed out to sea, sites of waste constitute "vigorous assemblages" of willed social amnesia and geobacterial intra-action.[149] Reilly acknowledges the irreducible relationality of waste. We do not externalize plastic waste; rather, we persist with (or through) it as the durable trace of an ephemeral desire. Single-use plastic might appear to "dematerialize" when we dispose of it, but it (and therefore we) will nonetheless continue to act on the environments it passes through for thousands of years as the plastic gradually breaks down. We are waste's companions in the slow violence of plastic's deep time:

(*for all averred, we had killed the bird*   [enter albatross
                                                       stand-in of choice[150]

Here Reilly rewrites Coleridge's Mariner's confession as an acknowl-edgment of collective responsibility. "[enter albatross" functions like a stage direction and, coupled with the glance at the albatross encounter in Melville's "The Whiteness of the Whale" that shadows it, summons the bird as an accusatory specter, like the ghost of Hamlet's father. Melville's narrator describes his first meeting with an albatross as a transcendent encounter: "A regal, feathery thing of unspotted whiteness . . . it uttered cries as some king's ghost in supernatural distress."[151] The reference to *Hamlet* figures this as a moment when "time is out of joint," ruptured by our willingness to make albatross bodies a sacrifice zone. Reilly's reference to landfill-buried waste as "still stunning all-color" calls to mind Chris Jordan's striking photographic series of albatross corpses filled with luridly colored plastic debris, taken on Midway Atoll.[152] Jordan has written that the carcasses are a "macabre mirror . . . reflect[ing] back an appallingly emblematic result of the collective trace of consumerism and runaway industrial growth." Significantly, the effect here is closer to Barad's notion of diffraction: "Choked to death on our waste, the mythical albatross calls upon us to recognise that our greatest challenge lies not out there, but in *here*." [153] Stacy Alaimo has observed how Jordan's images powerfully contrast the subdued colors of the decomposing seabirds with the bright, "eerily cheerful" pieces of plastic that have blocked the birds' digestive tracts and slowly starved them. The effect is a "strange jumbling" of scales of risk and precarity, as the most banal objects (lighters, bottle caps) wreak sublime damage on albatross populations.[154]

Thom van Dooren notes that Midway is a key breeding site for more than one-third of the global population of black-footed albatross and more than two-thirds of the world's Laysan albatross.[155] Ingested plastics have a devastating effect on these populations, particularly on chicks whose parents feed them plastic objects mistaken for food. Many perish of starvation or dehydration; those that survive are exposed to the damaging effects of phthalates and organochlorines, which reduce fertility and interfere with neurological and cell development. As apex predators, albatross carry significantly higher concentrations of toxic compounds than is present in their habitats.[156] It is here that, as van Dooren observes, temporalities and vulnerabilities "get messy": "Millions of years of albatross evolution—woven together by the lives and reproductive labors of countless individual birds—comes into contact with less than 100 years of human 'ingenuity' in the form of plastics and organochlorines discovered or commercialized in the early decades of the twentieth century."[157] This untimely, diffractive perspective is captured in Dickinson's poem "Hail," which opens,

> Hello from inside
> the albatross
> with a windproof lighter
> and Japanese police tape.[158]

Dickinson's poem gives voice to the intersection of time scales, deep and shallow, organic and synthetic, intra-acting in the body of the dead bird. The plastic debris slowly being revealed as the carcass rots hails us, which is to say that we are hailed by the durable trace world of our desires, drawing the subject of the poem's address into what Reilly calls our "shared materiality / among longtermheritage styrene."[159]

Reilly's work doesn't only expose the multispecies unevenness that attends life in the Anthropocene, a concern that will be examined in greater detail in the chapter to follow. Just as sacrifice zones occlude certain spaces as available for sacrifice, Reilly also examines how, in the Anthropocene, some human lives are also deemed expendable. The stories of plastic told in *Styrofoam* explore the uneven but widespread distribution of vulnerability through a densely entangled materiality. In effect, the central question posed by the collection as a whole regards the exposure associated with such a pervasive plasticity. *Styrofoam* offers a poetics of the risk society, exploring how multiple times, stories, and materialities intersect in the liveliness of deathless plastic. This is perhaps most evident in "Plastic Plenitude Supernatant," in which phrases excerpted from a scientific study of the possible presence of endocrine-disrupting chemicals in freeze-dried noodles intra-act with Reilly's elegy for Henrietta Lacks. Lacks was an African American woman who died of cervical cancer in Maryland in 1951. Cells extracted from Lack's biopsy, taken without her knowledge, were found to survive indefinitely outside her body. These cells formed the basis of HeLa, the first standardized cell line and still the most widely used cells in biomedical research. As Jayna Brown describes, HeLa revolutionized cell biology:

> Infinitely manipulable, [through HeLa] life could be perpetuated and altered both spatially and temporally. Life could be expressed in forms no longer bounded by individual organisms. Life could proliferate unrestricted by organismal cycles of birth and death. It was capable of reproducing outside heterosexual conception and could even transcend the notion of species. . . . Vitality had a newfound mobility.[160]

HeLa epitomizes, according to Brown, "the plasticity of life."[161] HeLa represents a form of simplification (of life to the cellular) as the basis for a radical ontological queering. Hannah Landecker notes that HeLa's distribution in laboratories across the world, from a single original specimen, introduces a "profound instability" to the concept of the human.[162] Yet the role of Henrietta Lacks in the story of HeLa was obscured for decades, with her own family remaining unaware of Lacks's legacy until 1975. HeLa's queering of life is therefore predicated on the erasure of other entanglements. Lacks died on a segregated ward, and the mass production of HeLa cells began in a facility where doctors were also conducting experiments on African American men with late-stage syphilis.[163] The deep time of plastic is crossed by what Paul Gilroy has called the "nanop-olitics" of biopolitical race-thinking.[164] In this, *Styrofoam* also gestures to the human lives given up to sacrifice zones—absorbed by indifference to rising sea levels, proliferating hazardous materials, drought, lost arable lands, and more extreme weather.

Reilly's poem is an elegy for immortal life. The poems ask, what constitutes mourning in a context of such deathlessness? Lacks is me-morialized with the phrase "petri dish to petri dish" rather than ashes to ashes, and Reilly's insistent repetition of Henrietta's name recovers the woman subsumed by the suprahuman range of HeLa.[165] Yet the elegy for Lacks becomes contaminated by other sources, interleaved with lines from the investigation of toxic noodles that used HeLa cells to examine the effect of synthetic chemicals on rat uteruses. The poem is acutely alert to the deadly irony here, given that it was Lacks's (forgotten) death from cervical cancer that led to the reproductive vitality of HeLa. In line with Jahan Ramazani's assertion that modern elegy is defined by the refusal to translate grief into consolation, "Plastic Plenitude Supernatant" probes the ethics of remaining unconsoled.[166] The use of open parentheses— "(ethereal replicant, Henrietta"; "(unearthly circlet, Henrietta"[167]— emphasizes an open-ended process, compounded by the closing comma in the final lines: "period period period period / Henrietta,"[168] Reilly's poem discloses how, as vulnerability is distributed through time—whether it is in terms of the racialized biopolitics of the HeLa cell line or of the toxic entanglements of what Reilly calls "our infinite plasticity prosperity plenitude"—incomplete mourning is a work of eternity.[169]

Following a visit to the former Union Carbide plant at Bound Brook, New Jersey (built by the inventor of oil-based plastics, Leo Baekeland, but sold to Union Carbide in 1939), Rebecca Altman reflects on "why we call industrial factories 'plants' in the first place":

> The related term, *factories,* is a shortening of *manufactories,* an exam-ple of how places are sometimes named according to what actions— manufacturing—are performed there. Hence smelters smelt. Paper mills mill paper. Ironworks work iron. *Refineries* refine petroleum. But *plants* don't follow the same logic. The corollary would be *plantations.*[170]

Both Peter Larkin and Evelyn Reilly expose how their subjects—the plantation forest and plastic material—are designed to conceal their histories: how plastic's durability (the "pre-" and "after-" lives of plastic objects that extend into very deep pasts and futures) exists in tension with and is typically obscured by its disposability and how the plantation forest, as a "precarious environment," creates an "opening into a mosaic of temporal rhythms and spatial arcs."[171] Scalability involves the translation of nature into a "pastless" resource; yet, as Tsing observes, "history plays havoc with scalability."[172]

Both poets engage with landscapes and materials that have been surrendered to the engines of consumption but that have nonetheless, remarkably, maintained their capacity to contribute to the project of world-making. Peter Larkin's open-field poetics explores the unruly difference that persists in blasted landscapes, characterized by rich intra-activity. Scarcity and entropy are not the preludes to exhaustion but rather the catalysts of renewed relationality. Through the diffractive sensibility expressed in Larkin's syntactically involute, coppiced verse, landscapes that have seemingly been silenced are revealed as still loud with their own semiotic being. Evelyn Reilly similarly examines the unruliness of plastic as a form of densely plotted intra-active relationality that binds us to the deep future. Marine plastic pollution produces multiple expressions of deep time: not only is plastic particulate contributing to changes to ocean chemistry that will persist into the very deep future but also it has driven the very recent evolution of specialist bacteria that feed off plastic waste.[173] Very slow and very rapid expressions of deep time intersect, encapsulating the formation of fossil fuels, the "presentism" of consumer culture, and the fast deep time of bacterial evolution, all within the compressed, plasticized poetics of "longtermheritage styrene." As Moore says, all resources are relational. Larkin's and Reilly's plantationocene poetics show how a lively experience of deep time, characterized by collaborative becoming and the "storied" aspect of matter, remains available even in the most depleted sacrifice zones.

Céleste Boursier-Mougenot, *Clinamen,* 2013 (detail). Porcelain, composition board, polyvinyl chloride, water pump, water heater, water. National Gallery of Victoria, Melbourne. Purchased NGV Foundation in memory of Loti Smorgon AO, 2013 (2013.568). Copyright Céleste Boursier-Mougenot/ADAGP, Paris. Licensed by VISCOPY, Sydney.

3

Swerve

THE POETICS OF KIN-MAKING

In 2013, sound artist Céleste Boursier-Mougenot suspended more than one hundred white porcelain bowls in a pool of cerulean blue water in the atrium of the National Gallery of Victoria in Melbourne. The water was heated to achieve the greatest possible acoustic resonance; colliding with one another as they bobbed about, the bowls created a chiming sound-scape. The title of the work, *Clinamen,* means "to swerve" and comes from Lucretius's *On the Nature of Things,* invoking the clustering motion of individual atoms. The installation was meant to imitate the swirl of celestial formations or atoms' erratic swoop. But it also suggests other, more creaturely images. The gently undulating bowls resemble a jellyfish bloom or else an enormous petri dish teeming with microbial life. It not only brings to mind the cosmic and the quantum but also resonates with the chthonic, the benthic, and the microbial.

The basis of this chapter is the contention that clinamen, the swerve that "sets off a ceaseless chain of collisions," as Stephen Greenblatt puts it, is the archetypal dynamic of what Donna Haraway calls kin-making.[1] We are "knotted beings," Haraway says, bound into densely woven re-lationships with other species across scales large and (very) small.[2] For Haraway, cultivating a sense of kinship with multispecies familiars is the most pressing obligation in an era of hemorrhaging biodiversity. But a turn toward the animal must also acknowledge and accommodate the fact that the animal other *turns away,* sometimes fleeing contact but always withdrawing into its impregnable *Umwelt.* As with Boursier-Mougenot's installation, a clinamen can lead to a collision or an entanglement. Despite these collisions, the bowls retain their integrity. Each remains intact; instead, as they turn into one another's path, each is simply diverted onto a new path. But in striking one another, by inclining toward one another, they collaborate in the performance of the soundscape, a pealing harmony that layers wave upon reverberating wave, each new swerve adding to the rich effect.

The swerve is the necessary turn or deviation that tangles life in knots of kin-making. Microbes acquire new genetic information through passing contact with other microbes or even the surrounding environment. Through donation, theft, invasion, or amnesty, microbes share themselves with a carnivalesque abandon. All multicellular life is indebted to the swerve of symbiosis. "Cellular interliving," Lynn Margulis tells us, "produced everything from spring-green blooms and warm, wet mammalian bodies to the Earth's global nexus."[3] Algal and plant chloroplasts contain genes that are the legacy of an ancient exchange in which one bacteria was absorbed by another, gradually evolving into organelles. From this first exercise in biotic "truce-forming" came chloroplasts, the basis for photosynthesis, and mitochondria, the source of energy for all complex respiring life-forms.[4] Life insistently swerves toward life.

Deborah Bird Rose writes of the "longing *for* others" as both a call from without to enter into connection and a reorienting pull from within the body. In the sway of "life's eros," she says, we are drawn "to turn toward self, to turn toward others."[5] In what follows, I examine Rose's notion of the turn in terms of the trope of the clinamen. To make kin is to incline toward another, relinquishing the illusion of the separate, bounded self for the startling reality of the self in community—that is, to perform a *clinamen,* a swerve between contexts. "One cannot make a world with simple atoms," Jean-Luc Nancy tells us. "There has to be a *clinamen.* There has to be an inclination or an inclining from one toward the other, of one by the other, or from one to the other."[6] This has particular resonance when it comes to the surprise and uncertainty that attends so many multispecies encounters: Alfred Jarry called clinamen "the unforeseen beast."[7] In light of this, I want to explore how clinamen also stands for a range of literary figures that can provide us with shapes for thinking about what a *poetics* of kin-making might look like. Tropes such as metaphor (in which an object is torqued into a new set of relations by the interplay of similarity and difference), apostrophe (whereby the speaker turns away to address another), or citation (which situates a poem in a chain of contiguous relations, some of which swerve away from their original contexts)—these forms of clinamen can provide frameworks for thinking about an intentional turn toward the nonhuman life that is also a turn back to the (newly strange) self.

Thinking with the swerve is not a matter of valorizing blind tangles or a utopian commingling. Difference always remains. Some swerves incline away, or toward with hostile rather than benign intent; others recoil. But as Boursier-Mougenot's *Clinamen* implies, the rebound can also be the basis of a collaborative encounter. We are already entangled with other life-forms, even before we intentionally incline toward them. It is, after all, a *sense* of kinship that we need to cultivate, for we in fact already do share kinship with countless nonhuman others. We are, according to Rose, "dense knots of embodied time."[8] Life is gifted not only through inheritance but also by uncountable coeval others that nourish each living creature throughout its life. Each individual is the outcome of an unfathomably dense and rich series of symbiotic relations and shared "coevolutionary histories."[9] We symbiotic beings *are* deep time. But this great planetary exercise in "world-making" is rapidly giving way to a "great unmaking," an unpicking of the knot.[10]

In nearly every ecosystem on Earth, the entanglement of life with death has been overtaken by what Rose calls "double death," the irrevocable loss of not only a single individual or even of all the living members of a given species but of the innumerable, branching iterations that would otherwise have spooled out along the animal's flight way. Double death is "the amplification of death, so that the balance between life and death is overrun, and death starts piling up corpses in the land of the living."[11] It is thought that the current rate of extinction is at least ten thousand times greater than the typical background rate of species attrition. A two degree Celsius rise above preindustrial global temperatures could mean an extinction rate for vertebrates as high as 58 percent.[12]

The profound rupture with ethical time represented by this catastrophic scale of loss is difficult to comprehend, but the entomologist

E. O. Wilson has produced a concise, if terrifying, summary: "The five previous major [extinction] spasms of the past 550 million years, including the end-Mesozoic, each required about 10 million years of natural evolution to restore," he writes. "What humanity is doing now in a single lifetime will impoverish our descendants for all time to come."[13] Perhaps more than any other environmental crisis, extinction pitches us into deep time: into awareness of the richness of our inheritance from the deep past, and the depleted legacy we will leave to the deep future.

In this context, to incline toward the nonhuman is a complex, compromised act. In 2008, the artist Caitlin Berrigan withdrew a small quantity of her own blood and poured it into a glass tray containing a common dandelion. For the plant blood is a rich source of nitrogen. But for Berrigan, who carries the hepatitis C virus, it is a site of trouble. Hepatitis C spreads through contact with infected blood. It is harmless to the dandelion, however, whereas the plant's roots and leaves are the basis of a therapeutic treatment of Berrigan's symptoms. Called *Life Cycle of a Common Weed,* the performance initiated what she called "a cycle of mutual cultivation."[14] The tangle of roots, tourniquets, and the tubes used in venepuncture all gesture toward the kind of "tentactularity" Haraway advocates as the principal ethic of the Chthulucene, her seriocomic alternative to the proliferating terminology of Anthropocene, Capitalocene, and so on. Sinuous, branching, and adaptive, life in the Chthulucene is irreducibly collaborative, "always partnered all the way down," winding into "knots of species co-shaping." But the reciprocal exchange also produces a negotiated "we" through the management of asymmetric relations of risk and repair: as Berrigan acknowledges, the exchange relies on the death of the plant. *Life Cycle* performs what van Dooren calls a "regime of violent-care,"[15] in which human nurturing of the nonhuman cannot be implemented outside systemic violence.

Weeds and the virus that causes hepatitis C are certainly what van Dooren and Rose call unloved and unwanted others, with whom we nonetheless often live in close proximity. Haraway's sample list of tentacular lives is dominated by the reviled and rejected: "cnidarians, spiders, fingery beings like humans and raccoons, squid, jellyfish, neural extravaganzas, fibrous entities, flagellated beings, myofibril braids, matted and felted microbial and fungal tangles, probing creepers, swelling roots, reaching and climbing tendrilled ones."[16] The wild shifts in scale and swerves between species bear witness to a deep and intimate, boundaryless strangeness. A poetics of kin-making embraces this carnival otherness. Loving the unloved other is also a displacement into strangeness precisely because it displaces us into ourselves. "We become who we are in the company of other beings," writes Rose;[17] but who we are—odd, thick knots of being—is perhaps not quite what we thought.

An Anthropocene poetics must address the knotty problem of love among knotted beings; the challenge of loving those creatures that seem to withdraw from or resist relation: the faceless, the swarming, or the microscopic. These life-forms stretch the knot of kin-making. If life is a form of *poiesis,* a mutual making, then to appreciate the depth of kin-making entanglements, we need an apocalyptic imaginary: one that can envision deep futures of world-making *and* world-unmaking. Mark Doty's poem "Difference" speaks to the troubling formlessness of jellyfish via the plasticity of metaphor; Sean Borodale's *Bee Journal,* which in the context of Colony Collapse Disorder rhapsodizes the life of the hive, performs an uncanny hailing of the hive-minded; and in *The Xenotext,* Christian Bök explores our symbiotic entanglement with microbial organisms by attempting to write an "eternal poem" in the genome of an unkillable bacterium. Each explores multispecies collaborations in terms of both their possibilities and their limits. In Doty's poem, the jellyfish inexorably swerves away from efforts to capture it in language; Borodale's collaboration with the bees turns away from conventional concepts of the "I" and the "now" of lyric poetry to be led by the rhythms of the hive; Bök explores how to write with bacteria in the language of their own genome, finding expression that defers to the bacteria's "linguistic being."[18]

The poetics of kin-making are collaborative, lovelorn, and unpredictable, thick with encounters both sensual and uncanny and fraught with risk. Sharing creaturely life involves, as Kelsey Green and Franklin Ginn put it, "opening ourselves up to the possibility that we are already given over to them and that we might have to change."[19] In this time of extinction, as the planet is dispossessed of biological and ecological richness, we need to embrace our own essential dispossession—that we are not separate but fundamentally coconstituted through others. We need to feel ourselves made strange to perceive how a once loudly abundant world is being made strange—silent, empty—to itself.

MARK DOTY: BALLOON, HEART, FLOWER, CONDOM

In June 2011, only four months after the tsunami that destroyed the Fukushima nuclear power station, a massive bloom of moon jellyfish forced a shutdown at Simane nuclear plant in western Japan. That same month, Torness nuclear power plant, approximately fifty kilometers outside of Edinburgh, undertook a precautionary shutdown after a similar mass jellyfish influx. The Orot Rabin electrical power station in Hadera, Israel, was forced to close by a jellyfish bloom in July, as was a Florida nuclear power plant the following month. Power plants are often situated near the oceans because of their need for large quantities of cool water. The closures occurred because, instead, vast numbers of jellyfish blocked the plants' filtration systems. This "bloom of blooms," occurring in the shadow of the devastation at Fukushima (which itself aroused anxious memories of Chernobyl), raised lurid fantasies of "jellygedon."[20] "Globe globe globe globe" is the opening line of Les Murray's "Jellyfish," neatly encapsulating the creatures' slow pulse and globular form; read in light of the threat of jellyfish-instigated nuclear apocalypse, Murray's imagist poem also anticipates contemporary anxieties of a world dominated by these fearfully strange beings.[21]

The rather vaguely defined group of creatures broadly known as jellyfish (which includes more than two thousand species of cnidarians, ctenophores, and tunicates)[22] are an immensely ancient life-form. There is fossil evidence that jellyfish swam in Precambrian oceans around 540 million years ago and possibly that they stretch back up to 640 million years, to the pre-Ediacaran period.[23] The notion that a life-form that has existed essentially unchanged since the Precambrian might be able to disrupt the operation of twenty-first-century nuclear power stations, and even release radioactive material into the very deep future, gives a new twist on the combination of "material effects, psychic tension, and sensory confusion" that Joseph Masco calls the "nuclear uncanny."[24] The fear is that what Anthony Richardson has called a "jellyfish joyride"—a wave of anthropogenic effects, including overfishing, eutrophication, ocean acidification, species translocation, and an increase in hard substrate— might carry marine ecosystems "back to the future."[25]

Some marine scientists have suggested that jellyfish may be synanthropic, direct beneficiaries of interactions with humans.[26] Nutrient runoff from heavily industrialized coastlines can induce phytoplankton blooms, increasing jellyfish food supplies, whereas overfishing and intensive trawling of the seafloor has reduced competition for resources and jellyfish predators. More acidic oceans soften the shells of many crustaceans, but jellyfish are significantly more tolerant of hypoxic conditions, and warm water may even trigger reproduction in some species. Humans have inadvertently moved jellyfish around the world for centuries in the ballast water of ships, stirring up new ecosystems, and the rise of the energy industry has provided a vast range of additional hard surfaces for jellyfish polyps to attach to, from oil platforms to offshore wind farms.[27] None of these factors alone causes jellyfish blooms, but they may act synergistically.[28] Elizabeth Johnson notes that jellyfish flourishing carries a bleak warning about the state of the oceans more generally: thriving in conditions that are harmful to most species, jellyfish blooms indicate that the oceans are increasingly inhospitable to the majority of marine life.[29]

Archetypal tentacular beings, jellyfish have become thickly entangled with the kinds of oceans humankind is creating. This is despite the profound difficulties we seem to have in identifying with them. Alternately visible and invisible, the same factors that make jellyfish difficult for marine scientists to trace also make them difficult to see with eyes of love. Jellyfish lack a center upon which human attention and care can gain purchase. They do not have eyes or anything resembling a face; they don't even have brains, possessing instead a diffusely arranged "nerve net." No center implies no self; as Jean Sprackland wonders in "The Currency of Jellyfish," "What must it be like / to have no bones, no guts, just that cloudy blue inside you?"[30] Stacy Alaimo notes that it is because of this saturation in "the cloudy blue" that jellyfish seem to "float beyond human comprehension." Borrowing from Jacques Rancière, she observes that "jellyfish—being watery—exist at the edge of the 'visible, the sayable, and the thinkable,' barely distinct from the seas that surround them, existing as flowing, pulsing, gelatinous, and just barely organized bodies. Jellies somehow live as the very element that surrounds them."[31]

Jellyfish are the archetypal unloved other, either ignored and unseen, or figured as abject substances (snot, slime, gloop). As Eva Hayward points out, however, this radical difference is accompanied by "shared histories [and] consequences."[32] Despite their seeming indistinctness, jellyfish bring the challenge of loving the unloved other, and of the poetics of kin-making, into sharp focus.

In Mark Doty's "Difference," the "perplexing liquidity" of jellyfish becomes the entire focus, or problem, of the poem.[33] The opening simile ("like schools of clouds") conjures a sense of flux and loose organization (compare Alaimo's "barely organized bodies"), after which the poem founders abruptly on the point of naming an affinity: "Is it right," Doty wonders, also to call jellyfish—"these elaborate sacks / of nothing"—*creatures*?[34] Almost as soon as it is taken up, the task of naming the jellyfish threatens to inflict defeat on the poem. The question could equally have to do with ethics as with accuracy: what claim do jellyfish make on us? It is not incidental that Doty fails to complete the phrase, "a dozen identical—," because it is in part the jellyfishes' sameness, the sense of mass replication subsuming the individual animal, that makes it so difficult to admit a creaturely affinity, a sameness, that emphasizes their profound difference from us.

Doty's poem drifts through a series of short stanzas composed of two or three beat lines, pulsing through position and counterposition as the animal becomes a balloon, a heart, and a flower, a condom, a plastic purse, and a parasol. Each image trembles on the edge of something else: the balloon, impossibly, is open at both ends, like a heart; the heart breathes, filling with air like a balloon; the flower bears a pulse. In the manner of Kate Rigby's notion of "negative ecopoetics," "within which . . . '[p]oetry sings the sayable world, but so as to let it be beyond every name,'"[35] Doty's jellyfish seems always on the cusp of swerving into a new shape until the creature is lost behind the parade of tropes. Paul Ricoeur argues that metaphor, as a "work of resemblance," is also a "semantic innovation" achieved through "a change in the distance between meanings,"[36] a weft and warp that resembles the flux unfolding in the poem. Endlessly malleable, the jellyfish becomes simply "the stuff / of metaphor."[37]

Metaphor is a form of clinamen, a swerve in thought that produces a new "knot" or cluster of understanding—a resolution of some form—without losing a sense of abiding difference. According to Ricoeur, metaphor negotiates what is like and what is unlike within a single form, through which "one must continue to identify the previous incompatibility through the new compatibility."[38] Metaphors are expressions of the malleability of language and perception, figures that draw entities into congregations of difference and relation (Erich Auerbach traces "figures" to *figura,* meaning "plastic form").[39] Figures, according to Haraway, are also where "the biological and literary or artistic come together with all the force of lived reality" and thus a key element of thinking about "world-making entanglements."[40] Jonathan Culler has observed that the figurative, which includes those "effects of language that exceed, deform, or deviate from the code," creates "opportunities for new turns,"[41] such as a swerve into a new kind of multispecies relation. This, for Culler, is the main work of the lyric, to multiply those figures to which we are urged to listen and respond.[42] But cnidarians represent, if anything, a mode of hyperfigurative being. Jellyfish are perhaps the most plastic of all animals. Their cells can be reproduced as any particular cell type in their bodies via a process called transdifferentiation: stinger cells become cells that form part of the bell, or vice versa. Under certain conditions, one species, the so-called immortal jellyfish or *Turritopsis dohrnii,* can change from its adult form back into juvenile polyps.[43] Doty's poem shows how the problem of *inclining toward* jellyfish is defined by the animal's excessive plasticity, its *swerve away* from language.

Balloon, heart, flower, condom, and parasol are metaphors for the jellyfish's orbicular form. But they also work *metonymically* as a parade of sentimentally romantic and sexual points of reference hinting at a desire for connection with the animal. The restless sequence, however, points to something that evades capture. The jellyfish continually approaches and retreats throughout the poem, blooming into new forms as each old trope collapses. What emerges is a kind of diffraction pattern. Metonymy diffracts, bending away from the linear and self-same to reveal, as Haraway puts it, "where the effects of differences appear."[44] As Hayward notes, diffraction is, etymologically, "the action of turning, or state of being turned, away from a straight line or regular path."[45] In their shape-shifting, undulant materiality, jellyfish are, she says, "living, respiring, metamorphosing diffraction patterns, [in] a constant state of transposing, becoming, and troping."[46] But it also describes the dynamic inherent to any poetics of kin-making: a turn toward the animal, an inclining toward the reality of shared concerns and collaborative world-making even while the animal itself turns away from any fixed shape. Working one final time through each trope in the series (balloon, flower, condom, etc.), the poem ends with a synesthetic invitation to *hear* the changed shape of the mouth that voices each trope, "so full / of longing for the world."[47]

Despite the effort to fit the jellyfish's strangeness into a familiar form, the animal itself recedes, leaving behind simply a mouth shaping globular "O" sounds, undulating like the jellyfish and pulsing with longing for it. This implied "O" that closes the poem is both a cry of longing and the "O" of apostrophic address. The poem hails the animal, which nevertheless floats away in a sea full of objects (balloon fragments, plastic waste) whose resemblance to it poses a fatal difference to other creatures (such as leatherback turtles, many of which choke on plastic bags because, in water, they resemble jellyfish). Ultimately, Doty's poem leaves us with a series of figures through which the jellyfish withdraws, only to reemerge as a sign of the way human actions are making the oceans not only more hospitable to jellyfish but increasingly hostile to other forms of marine life.

SEAN BORODALE: WRITING AT THE HIVE

In 2006, without warning, western honeybee workers began to vanish at an astonishing rate, leaving their hives to starve. One-third of all colonies were lost; beekeepers lost one-third of their hives again in 2012–13, by which time an estimated 10 million hives had failed.[48] Colonies were affected worldwide, wherever *Apis mellifera* are used as commercial pollinators. Alison Benjamin and Brian McCallum note that five million bees disappeared in Croatia within forty-eight hours.[49]

Colony collapse disorder (CCD), as the phenomenon became known, has a truly calamitous potential. The United Nations estimates that of the one hundred crops grown for human consumption, seventy-one are pollinated by bees, constituting approximately 90 percent of global yield.[50] In the United States alone, bees support a $15 billion agricultural industry.[51] A total collapse in honeybee colonies would have disastrous consequences for our capacity to feed ourselves (not to mention for the many other creatures whose food supplies depend on wild pollination). The possible causes are all linked to the simplifications of industrialized agriculture: malnutrition from the monoculture crops the bees are used to pollinate; the loss of genetic diversity as a result of selective breeding; disruption caused by transporting hives long distances to pollinate new farms; a pest known as the varroa mite; and neonicotinoids, a class of pesticide widely used in Western commercial agriculture that acts as a neurotoxin, impairing worker bees' ability to navigate. The most likely cause is a combination of factors, but bees' sensitivity to neonicotinoids led to a European Union–wide ban in 2013.

Much remains uncertain about CCD. Since 2013, fears of the "beep-ocalypse" have faded,[52] as the rates of CCD have declined but not stopped completely. As with the anticipated "jellygedon," it can be difficult to distinguish between genuine cause for alarm and the sublime appeal of incipient-extinction narratives. Nonetheless, CCD has revealed the complex and unappreciated relationship we have with bees. It made newly visible an animal that had tended to remain unobserved,[53] but the bees that materialized through CCD are not the bees of popular imagination—less the "festive spirit of nature" (as Freya Matthews describes the platonic bees in Maurice Maeterlinck's influential *The Life of the Bee*)[54] than dense knots of labor, technology, violence, and love.

In the menagerie of unloved others, insects hold a special place. They are, according to Eric Brown, "a kind of Other not only for human beings but for animals and animal studies as well."[55] Although not unloved per se, bees have largely appeared to us as the vehicle of metaphors about ourselves. Honeybee social organization has furnished idealized images of cooperation, sacrifice, and civic responsibility through successive ages. Virgil called the hive "a tiny / Republic that makes a show well worth . . .

admiration";[56] Shakespeare's *Henry V* counsels that honeybees "teach /
the act of order to a peopled kingdom."[57] The "distributed intelligence"
of the colony, subsuming innumerable, mingled life-forms to the agency
of a single "superorganism," exemplifies the resilience of the *socius*; but
however we might turn toward the bee, it also recoils from our attention.
Rather like the jellyfish, the honeybee "defies our habitual categories of
identity," as Matthews puts it.[58]

This failure to see the bee has historically been bound up in regimes
of violent-care. Virgil describes clipping the wings of queen bees to prevent swarming. Hugh Raffles notes how Karl von Frisch, who received
the Nobel Prize in 1973 for his discovery of the honeybee dance language
and who saw his bees as "personal friends," would "lovingly (with another
love), painstakingly (with a profound patience), and delicately (with such
safe hands) snip their antennae, clip their wings, slice their torsos, shave
their eye bristles, glue weights to their thoraxes, and carefully paint shel-
lac over their unblinking eyes," all in the name of a better understanding
of the bee.[59] Jake Kosek enumerates how this appropriation of the honeybees' evolved behaviors has constituted a remaking of the honeybee,
including transformations to its exoskeleton, nervous system, digestive
tract, and collective social behavior. Worker bees in industrial hives are
one-third larger and more docile than their wild cousins, but their lives
are 15 percent shorter.[60] The modern bee is a conglomeration of imposed
adaptations, like Frankenstein's pollinators. Bees are now used in some
parts of the United States as biomonitors for toxic materials.[61] "Bees are
becoming more human," Kosek summarizes, "in that human sentiments
become part *of* the bee and humans come to know the world in part *through*
the bee."[62]

Virgil's *Georgics* demonstrates that humans have been entangled with
bees for a very long time. One theory suggests that human evolution
was in part due to our consumption of honey, providing critical energy
for an enlarged brain.[63] To show concern over the "becoming human"
of honeybees does not therefore connote a kind of reductionist vision
of the "pure bee." But we need to recognize that our shared histories,
longue durée knots of interspecies becoming, include forms of violent-care.
Less the *beneficiaries* of human contact than jellyfish, honeybees used in

commercial pollination will nonetheless now carry the traces of their interaction with humans along their evolutionary flight ways. Barring the apocalyptic collapse forecast by CCD, we are partnered with bees into the very deep future.

Sean Borodale's *Bee Journal* explores how to achieve a thickening of relations with bees in the midst of this great thinning of biodiversity. The collection records the poet's first eighteen months as an apiarist, including the death of his first hive, and culminates with the acquisition of a replacement colony. The blunt, descriptive title aligns it with a category of titles that, as Paul Muldoon suggests, "act as signposts" for the reader's attention,[64] highlighting that this is a very particular kind of collection, a hybrid of lyric poem and private recollection, with, therefore, a very particular sense of time. Each poem is a separate, dated entry: sometimes couched in the technical language of apiculture, even its banalities; at others, Borodale's inquisitiveness and developing obsession with the bees are framed by a freewheeling lyricism that moves off into the uncanny or associative, by turns curious, ecstatic, and anxious.

The vast majority were written directly at the hive; to do so was, Borodale has confirmed, a very deliberate act, a means to connect the "active, physical, bodily, temporal, visceral process" of writing with the hives' urgency.[65] The book is, he says, "verse written in the moment." Since 2003, Borodale has developed the "lyrigraph" as a means to capture the sense of a moment that would otherwise evaporate. Lyrigraphs are short verses that have a documentary quality, composed and edited in direct contact with the moment they describe, in the midst of what Borodale has called "the potent present." "I have tried to think of this term as specifically different to ordinary everyday time," he writes. "It is *intended* time, for language on the brink of transformation."[66] Borodale's lyrigraphs make plain how the lyric now is pregnant with other times. The poems in *Bee Journal* were composed over two years in a handwritten diary; other than removing pieces here and there, they were not subsequently edited, allowing Borodale to note the "slow changes and taperings, [the] adjustments," that constitute the time of the hive.[67] Each lyrigraph and each bee is a "weird filigree of livid minute," threaded to its own rhythms and seasonality.[68]

Bee Journal is, therefore, a highly recursive text, attuned to the microdifferences within repetitive action. Its primary interest lies in being present and available to a very *other* sense of time. Many of the lyrigraphs are written in the present tense, but the immediacy of the journal format, framed as the rendering of a direct and specific encounter, only exacerbates "the oddity of the lyric time of enunciation." Lyric poems are written for repeat performance, once to be resung, latterly to be reread. The peculiar *now* of the lyric, Culler tells us, is therefore "not timeless, but a moment of time that is repeated every time the poem is read."[69] Presented as a journal, Borodale's collection of lyrigraphs enacts the same iterability— of serially returning to the same point of exposure—within which other time scales circulate. The "lyrical time" Borodale pursues is, he says, "a time-state rather than a tense," an "absolute present" that also carries "a sense of stretching and . . . looped tangling," in which "deep time and the lyrical times co-exist."[70]

A geologic sensibility plays out alongside the seasonal rhythms of the hive and Borodale's daily observances. This is so from the very first encounter: when he collects the hive, he observes the air "ancient with thin flecks" of bees like glints in mica.[71] He recounts how much of his time initially was spent "just listening to them . . . putting my ear to the back of the hive and just listening, and I had a very strong sense . . . that in listening I was really listening to the whole evolutionary tract, the song. A fifty million year old song."[72] The brief life of each bee, only a few weeks long, "cycl[es] up from millennia's blackness"[73]—writing at the hive becomes an exercise in tracing the braiding of times across wildly differing scales.

For instance, "27th May: Geography" expresses the disorientation induced by the bees' arrival, packing the walls and roof of Borodale's house. Writing at the hive is, he states, "a crowded moment,"[74] an experience that comes forcefully through in the poem's stress-packed lines and swarming points of reference. The opening stanza is boldly trochaic, darting through a series of subordinate clauses as the poem's attention tries to keep pace with the brimming bees. It resolves, however, in the opening of the second stanza, into a full, spondee-rich line ("And they rig crack, lump, recess, ridge").[75] This clustering of stresses, up to six in

a line, becomes a characteristic feature. Checking the brood frame reveals "living small bulbs of eye: note, bee glow"; winter honey is a "solid
broth / of forest flora full of fox"; the comb is like "the grain of a moon, a
spoon-back of pale no one"; and the bees themselves are a "*small irritated
power-tool shape of sound.*"[76] It is as if the only way to keep up with "each
wing touch, leg rub, dance" is through the "congestion of language."[77] The
poems in *Bee Journal* often convey a sense of overstimulation and how
"being in the middle of a colony is a radicalization of all the senses."[78] This
is emphasized by the refrain "and they rig it" in "27th May: Geography."
"Rig" derives from the Norwegian *rigga,* meaning "to wrap" or "to bind
up." The anaphora binds together hive, house, and environs in a weave
of different temporalities—the fleeting moment of the "last floodlit bit
of daylight" and the "commune of a memory" that reaches back into the
deep past. The colony stitches its own "net of flightways" over the house,
"turning this house to align with yours."[79] The disorientation of the bees'
arrival is the disorientation of coming to realize oneself as a knotted being,
entwined with the flight ways of numerous animal others.

While Borodale's lyrigraphs don't have a fixed metrical shape, in *Bee
Journal,* they do possess a particular and very strong kind of rhythmic
sense. In one respect, the habitual return to stand before the hive provides
what Richard Cureton calls "rhythmic theme,"[80] ensuring a sense of rhythmic continuity in a sequence whose discontinuous moments nonetheless
compose a single poem.[81] But *Bee Journal* also exhibits something less
tangible. Although the poems were not revised, they were "premeditated"
in the sense of preparing to engage with what Borodale calls "the theatre
of the hive": "I considered how I wanted to meet it and be in it and be with
it. . . . So when I come to write them I haven't already created phrases but
I've created a kind of tone, which in some way holds the phrases."[82] This
"pretone" resembles what Henri Meschonnic calls "third rhythm," "the
subjective character of rhythm" that sits somewhere between the thinking
mind and the speaking voice.[83] Marjorie Perloff detects "third rhythm" in
Samuel Beckett's characteristically stilted but insistent speech rhythms,
both "discontinuous and repetitive, . . . a kind of shorthand by means
of which the human consciousness tries to articulate what it perceives

and remembers."[84] Something of this quality of "mentalese"—of a mind striving to capture what is fleeting but continuous—is also present in the rhythms of the lyrigraphs, whose time signature is "interruptedness."[85]

Through its rhythmic shifts, "27th May: Geography" swerves between the time of the bee and the lyrical "present." *Trochee,* which signifies a "running foot," has its roots in the Greek *choree,* "belonging to the dance"[86] and might perhaps bring to mind the waggle dance of the honeybees, which is such an essential part of their own particular time-sense.[87] Dances are, as J. A. Haldane puts it, "at once histories and prophesies."[88] Von Frisch stated that bees "carry an unbreakable watch in their bodies."[89] As Muldoon observes, spondee "has at its heart the idea of duration, the duration of the pouring of a drink-offering."[90] The colony's buzz, with its continuous, droning emphasis, also has a spondaic quality, but the duration is a much longer one, "the fifty million year old song" that plays continually through the hive, with its "weight measurable by thickenings of sound."[91] Something close to the "thick time" of Seamus Heaney's lyrics also inhabits Borodale's verses. "I am interested in the thickness of time," he says, "that it achieves different viscosities as we tune ourselves or are retuned."[92] For Meschonnic, rhythm was the source of meaning—*la signifcance*;[93] for Borodale, it signifies the thickness of time and the viscosity of the lyric now, in which things adhere, cluster, and bond.

Any disorientation is, of course, also a reorientation—a turn toward a new direction. Culler notes that the etymology of apostrophe, where the poet turns from the audience to address a new person or entity, "emphasises the turning rather than the anomalous address."[94] Apostrophic address can therefore be a form of clinamen, a turn toward a new structure of relation. In performing his clinamen, his turn toward the bees, Borodale also encounters the unbreachable resistance of a compelling but, finally, alien *Umwelt.* The poem figures each bee as a firing synapse in a restless hive mind that overwhelms the poet. Caught in the hives' flaring buzz, he hesitates—"I have to say," "I said"—betraying a voice unsure of its ground.[95] Mutlu Blasing describes how, although the speaking "I" gives shape and action to the poem, it is ultimately no more than "the sound of intention" made to cohere by the force of rhythm. Rhythm "sounds . . . an intention to mean," to be "intelligible to a 'you' in time."[96]

But the challenge in *Bee Journal* is how a single lyric "I" can "become with many."[97] To address an individual bee in the midst of this activity is impossible, but to address the hive ("small, small, small sounds composing one") stretches the limits of apostrophic address.[98] According to Culler, apostrophe, which seeks "above all . . . to establish relations between self and other," can at times lead to a "radical interiorization," either "parcel[ling] out the self to fill the world" or drawing in "what might have been thought external."[99] But in "27th May: Geography," the enfolding of self and other—"in *your* trance *I* had to say, this / an afternoon of lifetimes tightening into knots"[100]—leaves Borodale curiously peripheral in his own poem.[101]

There is, of course, an element of fantasy to this. *Bee Journal* is a peculiarly lovelorn book. Borodale himself suggests that "it does, in a way, become a kind of love story."[102] At times, in the face of such a recalcitrant interlocutor, Borodale's ardent desire for the bees resolves into lyrical fallacy, claiming to hear the "shivering tissh" of a bee landing on the "unsteady cymbal of [a] flower's radial."[103] His attentiveness to the minutiae of hive life is rhymed inversely by the hive's busy absorption in itself, "impervious with process," and thus the poems are preoccupied by the distance between them.[104] "In" is a recurring preposition, with Borodale peering into the hive's dark spaces or wondering if the bees are at home or foraging. But as the bees become a more substantial presence, their keeper wanes: gloomily longing when the colony winters; tuned toward a kind of diffractive being ("I am two beekeepers," he observes, "just in phase").[105] He turns repeatedly toward the bees, but they do not turn to him. To this extent, the unevenness that marks the relationship between bee*keeper* and *kept* bees is reversed. The bees occupy the sum total of Borodale's attention. Almost nothing of the rest of his life—other relationships or occupations, not even the wider environs of the house unless encountered through or in relation to the hive—is allowed to intrude on the intimacy he assiduously pursues. Days and weeks pass between entries; in many poems, the bees are a longed-for absence. It is as if Borodale concedes to the bees the authority to determine whether or not a poem will be written: "This is I," writes a bee wandering over a page of Borodale's journal.[106]

Many lyrigraphs are overtaken by the bees, their rhythms determining where the poems' attention is directed. *Bee Journal* as a whole thrums with the noise of the hive, "trying out *its* harmonics."[107] In "17th October: Audio Recording," Borodale describes using a microphone to try to capture its "unique vertigo," in "a fizzing spaghetti- / junction of swerves."[108] What is partly an impossible exercise in parsing the language of the bee becomes also an intra-active form of composition, both bees and beekeeper "making new language out of cross-lapsed phrase."[109] Harold Bloom's theory of how one writer exercises influence over another turns on the swerve of the clinamen, what he calls "poetic misprision": the willful misinterpretation of a precursor.[110] This is how poetry has always renewed itself. But it is perhaps worth also keeping in mind the association in Greek between *meli* (honey) and *melos* (to sing), and that the Hebrew word for "bee," *debvorah,* derives from the base verb form *dabvar,* "to speak."[111] Borodale's hesitation over the question of lyric address—of who turns to speak to whom in the poem—frames *Bee Journal* as a kind of multispecies misprision, an inevitable mishearing of the bees' song that yields an often anxious, beseeching suite of poems.

Borodale has spoken of how Bruno Latour's phrase, "the slight surprise of action," influenced him when writing *Bee Journal.* We are, Latour states, "slightly overtaken" by "the *clinamen* of our action. . . . I never act; I am always surprised by what I do."[112] Any given action is a composite of acts that are the properties of innumerable humans and nonhumans, reaching back into deep time: as Latour says, "we hourly encounter hundreds, even thousands, of absent makers who are remote in time and space yet simultaneously active and present."[113] For Borodale, honey is perhaps the archetype of what Latour calls "congealed labour," containing scent- and flavor-traces of wood, rot, sweat, the blood of mites, and also "something / human."[114] Honey is a composite of lives, actions, matter, and inheritances (later, he describes a pot of honey as "a ghost of a going-on").[115] Crucially, the human is present in this spectrum of strange tastes, a dense agglomeration of influences and processes. His cultivation and consumption of the honey is also punctuated by his anxious sense of inequality. As Catriona Sandilands observes, honey can provide "a sort of taste experience of bee *Umwelt,*" but it also carries a political flavor:

"how we organise environments for pollination registers not only in bee welfare, but also in human taste."[116] Although his bees are wild foraging, their honey is nonetheless the product of an economic arrangement. The enfolding of human and nonhuman is not a flat or neutral process but a highly uneven one marked by the exigencies of violent-care. Richard Nimmo has remarked on honey's ambiguous cultural status, as both "given by nature and manufactured";[117] for Freya Matthews, it is the "poetically delivered" outcome of the hives' "inter-coherence of ends"—"a system in which each individual pursues its own ends yet in doing so satisfies exactly the needs of the others in the system."[118] In other words, honey is the end of the contradictory poem of kin-making. This viscosity extends to the form of the journal itself. Borodale recalls his surprise, on revisiting the notebooks in which the journal was kept, "to see how much had been marked in the pages other than my handwriting, *things had added themselves.*"[119] Other actors play their part and make their mark; literally and figuratively, the lyrigraphs are sticky with the evidence of different lives and happenings.

The question of how to love the hive, then, converges with how to manage it. Borodale's acts of care—dusting the colony with icing sugar to guard against varroa infestation—are also interventions, edged with the violence of managing others. He expresses a deep fascination with the queen, repeatedly the object of anxious searches; yet he also permits a DEFRA inspector to clip her wings to prevent swarming. "To keep" conveys a range of meanings within the ambit of violent-care: hold, cherish, nurture, or capture, constrain, possess. Each carries risks. His power over the fate of the hive is counterpointed by an acute sense of vulnerability to their loss. Borodale kept the journal in the shadow of CCD. "Bees in other hives out there are dying in droves," he records.[120] But despite his efforts, the hive is overcome by a varroa infestation. Its loss compounds the disorientation of kin-making. The house is "dishevelled" by grief; yet there is irony, too, in the fact that the colony's death allows the consummation of Borodale's desire to see inside the hive and to handle the queen. Matthews has suggested that, in mourning CCD, we enter into an expanded grief. "In grieving at the disappearance of the honeybee," she writes, "I am grieving for the diminishment of the biosphere."[121] But *Bee*

Journal balances this more expansive, multispecies ethics with a deeply felt concern for the bee itself as a densely knotted being whose swerving flight way intersects so richly and painfully with Borodale's own. Caught between beekeeper and "bee-friend" (a phrase that also recurs throughout *Bee Journal*), Borodale continually runs up against the problem of keeping, finding ultimately that what he keeps is, as he has said himself, "a state of vulnerability."[122]

CHRISTIAN BÖK: THE ETERNAL POEM

In 2003, Pak Wong of the Pacific Northwest National Laboratory speculated that, in the face of the need to preserve vital data against planetary catastrophe, bacterial DNA could be used as a stable repository of encoded information.[123] To demonstrate his theory, Wong encoded the lyrics to *It's a Small World After All* (written by the Sherman Brothers in 1963, as a jokey response to the Cuban missile crisis) in the DNA of two bacteria: *E. coli*, and *Deinococcus radiodurans*, an extremophile bacterium that can withstand extraplanetary conditions.[124] DNA-encoded information would be extraordinarily resilient, protected by life's capacity to replicate. Wong ventured that certain, particularly hardy organisms, such as cockroaches, could provide living repositories for hundreds of millions of years.[125]

Wong's was not the first attempt to exploit the "indestructible" information storage potential of DNA. This was in 1986, when MIT researcher and artist Joe Davis inserted a crude picture of *algiz,* the "life rune" in Germanic script meant to connote a female Earth, in a sample of *E. coli.* There have since been many similar endeavors. The enciphered material is often poised between hubris and an awareness of ecological fragility. In 2003, a team led by Sylvestre Marillonnet introduced a line from book II of Virgil's *Georgics* ("nec vero terrae ferre omnes omnia possunt" [Neither can every soil bear every fruit]) in the genome of a genetically modified flower;[126] and in 2010, scientists at the J. Craig Venter Institute encoded a quote from James Joyce's *A Portrait of the Artist as a Young Man* ("To live, to err, to fall, to triumph, to recreate life out of life") in a sample of DNA (and subsequently incurred the censure of the notoriously protective Joyce Estate).[127] In 2011, George Church of Harvard University encoded a

JavaScript program and his own latest book in synthetic DNA; the following year, Nick Goldman and Ewan Birney of the European Bioinformatics Institute encoded a clip of Martin Luther King's "I Have a Dream" speech, a PDF of Watson and Crick's paper on the helical structure of DNA, and the complete sequence of Shakespeare's sonnets;[128] and in 2013, Davis (again) re-created the Tree of Knowledge by encoding a page of Wikipedia in a four-thousand-year-old strain of apple.[129] In 2017, Yaniv Erlich and Dina Zielinski created a microscopic cabinet of curiosities by encoding a complete computer operating system, Claude Shannon's foundational 1948 paper on information systems, a fifty-second silent film, images of the plaques placed on board the Pioneer 10 and 11 spacecraft, and a fifty dollar Amazon gift card, in a tiny speck of DNA.[130]

These experiments, which seek to inscribe a human presence in living matter that will persist into the very deep future, celebrate humanity's capacity to act within what Jay Clayton calls "genome time": a "present made to contain every possible permutation of time as a legible system of signs."[131] Clayton's textual metaphor corresponds with a wider emphasis on textuality in genetic discourse. References to the genome as book, code, recipe, or blueprint to be edited, deciphered, or adapted are common in both scientific and popular representations of the genome, indicative of a desire to extract life from its compost of relations and render it a stable object we can intervene in or act on. In one sense, genome time and its expression in the work of Wong, Davis, and others is acutely Anthropocenic. Genome time is synchronic, fusing "the personal timescale of everyday life with the immense impersonal timescale of the species."[132] Its elastic temporality is thus open to an exploration of intergenerational ethics, posing questions about the kind of readable legacy we wish to hand down to future generations. But this elasticity always snaps back into a particular fixed position. In vaunting the capacity of human ingenuity to cheat deep time, both genome time and the experiments in DNA encryption depend on the genome as a self-contained repository of all possible evolutionary pasts and futures.

According to this view, life inheres in the genome to the exclusion of biological or environmental relations. Different futures may be only latent in genome time, in need of activation, but they are ultimately contained within the genome's own potential rather than in the potential of what lies beyond it and interacts with it. But this notion, that all times are inscribed in the perpetual present of the genome, puts life in a vacuum. Such "gene fetishism," as Haraway puts it, depicts the gene as inherently singular, "outside the lively economies of troping."[133] By contrast, Evelyn Fox Keller describes genes as "an exquisitely sensitive reaction (or response) mechanism";[134] for Haraway, "a gene is not a thing" but "a node of durable action where many actors, human and nonhuman, meet."[135] Stefan Helmreich refutes the textual metaphors that characterize DNA discourse, arguing that DNA at least ought to be understood "hypertextually, with meaning read out in relation, pragmatically, not written in beforehand."[136] What a gene "means" may be determined by factors that are exogenous to the DNA code, such as via lateral gene transfer or epigenetic influences. In contrast with van Dooren's concept of a species's individual flight way, which responds continually to the impress of environments and other beings as it threads its way through evolutionary time, genome time does not allow for "the unapologetic swerving of liveliness."[137] Life progresses *when it turns,* swerving into the path of other life; it advances via "the unexpected movement of matter,"[138] that is, via the *clinamen.*

In defiance of the long-term legacies of irradiated nuclear waste, a fossil record of mass extinction, and the global effects of climate change, Christian Bök's ongoing *Xenotext* experiment is an attempt to write an "eternal" poem in the genome of an extremophile bacterium.[139] *D. radiodurans,* "the dire seed, immune to radiation,"[140] can withstand exposure to gamma radiation more than one thousand times greater than the lethal dose for human beings. In 2002, NASA painted a layer of the bacterium on the payload of an MK-12 Black Brant Rocket and blasted it into space, where it was exposed to ultraviolet solar radiation at an altitude of 304 kilometers for more than six minutes; yet a viable colony returned to Earth with the rocket.[141] It was first detected in 1956, during U.S. military experiments in the use of ionizing radiation to sterilize tinned meat, making "the dire seed" another expression of Masco's nuclear uncanny.[142] There is presently no known way to kill it. The bacterium is so robust, Bök speculates, that it may outlast all other life on Earth and bear witness, one day in the deep future, to the death of the sun.[143] Inspired by the work of Wong and John

Davis, and transgenic artists such as Eduardo Kac, *The Xenotext* hails the aesthetic possibilities in genetic science, granting geneticists "the power to become poets in the medium of life."[144]

The Xenotext itself is a mutually enciphering pair of sonnets, "Orpheus" and "Eurydice." Bök wrote a computer program to select a viable cipher (ANY-THE 112) from nearly 8 trillion possibilities—one that would not only permit him to write "Orpheus" at the same time as "Eurydice" but also wouldn't alter the bacteria's genome when encoded as a protein. His method exploits the process of RNA transcription. Nucleotides, the basic units of deoxyribonucleic acid, appear in sets of three called codons, composed of combinations of four nucleobases: adenine (A), cytosine (C), guanine (G), and thymine (T). Bök selected twenty-six codons and assigned each a letter of the alphabet, thus enabling him to encode "Orpheus" into the genome of a bacterium. Because codons are instructions for translating DNA into ribonucleic acid (RNA), during which each nucleotide of DNA corresponds to another of RNA (with urasil [U] standing in for thymine), the microbe becomes an uncanny coauthor in the process. As the genetic sequence for "Orpheus" is fed through the ribosome (a kind of molecular translation machinery within living cells), the bacterium "reads" the original poem and uses it to create a protein that, when run through the ANY-THE 112 cipher, reemerges in katabatic fashion as a new poem, "Eurydice."[145]

Orpheus represents the principle of inspiration: according to Elizabeth Sewell, Orpheus is "poetry thinking itself."[146] His song could persuade all of nature, even stones, to bend to his will. In his *Sonnets to Orpheus,* Rilke eulogizes the poet's "formative song" that pours forth from "a mouth which else Nature would lack."[147] The Orpheus of Rilke, and much of literary tradition, represents an association of word and life that recalls the excesses of gene fetishism:

Breathing, invisible poem!

. . .

O Fountain mouth, your mouth that can respond
So inexhaustibly to all who ask
With one, pure, single saying.[148]

His indestructible lyric stands for the Xenotext itself. Like the severed head of Orpheus, which continued to lament as it floated away on the river Hebrus, Bök's intention is that the dire seed's song will sound into eternity. Julian Murphet finds a precursor to Bök's postulation of writing as a defense against "devouring Time" in Shakespeare's sonnets, which present the sonnet form "as a kind of selfish gene. The 'image' it contains is perfectly generic, empty, non-specific. . . . What matters is that it goes on writing itself, warding off competition and holding fast to its theme with adaptive ingenuity."[149] In Bök's case, the "self-substantial fuel" (which sustains the beauty of Shakespeare's young man and which the poet transmutes into his own capacity to make "monuments" by "my gentle verse")[150] is *D. radiodurans* itself, which owes its extraordinary resistance to decay to its capacity to repair damaged chromosomes without mutation.

Many critics have therefore read a vaulting gene fetishism in Bök's "apocalyptic conceptual poem":[151] for Ada Smailbegović, *The Xenotext* is conceptually reliant on metaphors of encryption that privilege a "'gene-centric' understanding of DNA" and replicate heteronormative biases;[152] John Charles Ryan worries that its investment in the notion of the archive undermines the project's more radical elements;[153] and Robert Majzels proposes that, while the project "imagines it is initiating a conversation," it problematically "interrupts the other's speech, the nucleotide's own poem,"[154] a poem that, presumably, would resist being read altogether. Both Ada Smailbegović and Nikki Skillman observe how the Xenotext itself exploits the erotic resonance of the sonnet by pairing what are implicitly masculine and feminine interlocking poems,[155] affirming what Judith Roof has identified as a heteronormative bias in DNA discourse.[156]

Bök does express a keen sense of wonder at the sublime miracle of "spontaneous, biochemical inscription" that preserves and furthers life.[157] DNA is celebrated as the "Alpha Helix," the title of the final sequence in the first volume of *The Xenotext*. However, his turn toward the bacterium is more open to the swerving, troping liveliness of kin-making than such critiques allow. It is "the little vortex that can torque / the course of evolution for every micrococcus"; "It embroiders us with error."[158] The kinetic, intra-active operations of the fabulous molecule are defined by what Roof calls "a logic of contiguity (or metonymy)," whereby "each site of interaction affects each other site."[159] In his "delirious catalogue" of "living poetic forms," life proceeds through collision, alliance, and ricochet — as "feedback loop" and "fractal globule," via torsions and vortices.[160]

Thus Bök's highly constrained poetics affirms a more lateral dynamic comparable to the aesthetics of interaction and interconnectedness in Peter Middleton's epigenetic poetics.[161] Most of all, these swerves occur through a series of misprisions, moments when the Xenotext intersects with a literary forebear. Both formally and with reference to specific poems and poets, the Xenotext sets off a "chain of literary collisions," swerving between intertexts and bearing their imprint, in a manner that is closer to the playful, generative information-sharing processes of lateral gene transfer than to the emphasis on vertical transmission and descent in DNA replication. Behind the apparent affirmation of a text-centric concept of life, the Xenotext subtly inclines to a livelier sense of human–microbial collaboration.

Bök's project is distinct from other attempts to encode information in living material precisely because of the focus on the art of writing: "Let us build not only a durable archive for storing such lyrics, but also *an operant machine for writing their echoes.*"[162] If such a statement leaves Bök open to accusations of mechanizing life, it also opens the project to other, uncanny influences. Although they are prewritten, the poems are determined by the bacteria's own biochemical responses. The Xenotext not only promises to echo into the deep future but also works through a collaborative aesthetic in which literary and biochemical echoes shape its meaning.

The Xenotext is a work of 'pataphysics, Alfred Jarry's "science of imaginary solutions"[163] that looks to invest scientific certainty with a measure of poetic irony. 'Pataphysical works turn away from the hubristic certainty of enlightenment science and embrace the capacity to be in the midst of uncertainties: 'Pataphysics, Bök says, "narrates not what is but what might have become. It inhabits the tense of the future perfect . . . a paradoxical temporality, in which what has yet to happen has already taken place."[164] However much the notion of an eternal poem might bring to mind the "silence and slow time" of Keats's "Ode on a Grecian Urn," Bök is less interested in timelessness than in *untimeliness.* For all its investment in scientific innovation, the Xenotext is "out of sync with its current moment in history."[165] It articulates an apocalyptic negative capability.

The first publication to come out of the project, *The Xenotext: Book 1,* is a mix of genetic primer and process-based, apocalyptic pastoral poetry, published in 2015. Book 1, the "Orpheus" volume, examines the pastoral past; book 2, which is yet to appear and will detail the outcomes of the project, is the "Eurydice" volume concerned with our "sci fi future."[166] Bök's earlier projects have also worked within excessive constraints. *Crystallography* (1994) was written in the geochemical "language" of minerals; in *Eunoia* (2001), he produced a sequence of five poem-chapters, each restricted to the use of a single vowel. Each work has pursued the generative potential in constraint, bearing out Perloff's assertion that constraint "tends towards multiplicity."[167] Despite its linguistic and biochemical restrictions, the Xenotext proves the weird durability of language. "Language is very robust," Bök has said. "Even under duress, it finds a way to say something uncanny, if not sublime."[168] Darren Wershler records that one early abandoned cipher, WOR-VIT 190, produced a pair of corresponding imagist poems: "tidal / words of life / copy song" and "roads / vital in song / pick life."[169] The pairing of key words even in these brief fragments yields a rich tide of meanings and associations that offer an ambivalent reflection on the Xenotext project. "Words" / "vital" and "life" / "song" evoke the text-fixation that insists on speaking of DNA in terms of languages and codes, but "pick" / "copy" hints at the way Bök's mode of composition concedes to *D. radioduran*'s unique biochemical "song."

Another way to put this is that Bök collaborates with the bacterium in terms of its particular semiotics. Bacterial communities are also meaning making. Bacteria can possess a form of inherited memory through cell differentiation or make use of a collective epigenetic memory (for example, in responding to antibiotics). In moments of stress, starved cells within a bacterial colony will emit a chemical signal; healthier bacteria use the information to interpret the overall well-being of the colony, on the basis of which each individual bacterium "votes" on whether the colony should sporulate. As Myra Hird summarizes, bacteria can converse, learn, deliberate, and evaluate;[170] that is, they possess what Walter Benjamin would call a distinctive "linguistic being."[171] Collaboration with such a partner is, Bök has affirmed, "a negotiation," akin to "trying to appease a little god."[172] "I actually have to generate these texts in response entirely to [the bacterium's] own constraints," he states. "I'm not telling it what to do. Its biological rules are in fact telling me what to do."[173] Despite the reliance on textual metaphors (which present the bacteria "reading" and "writing" the encoded poems), Bök's poems "address . . . life itself in its own language."[174]

The central dynamic of 'pataphysical work is the clinamen, what Bök calls deviance, which "finds a way to detour around things."[175] The Xenotext performs a series of swerves. In inclining toward an extremophile bacterium, Bök's work turns as well toward the very deep future. But it also makes a third turn, reaching back into literary history. Perloff has described how the key distinction between Language poetry and the constraint-based poetics of poets like Bök (what she calls "poetry by other means") lies in a kind of clinamen: a return to the literary tradition. For all its opposition to the conventions of lyric voice via the new sentence, Language poetry maintains, Perloff states, a belief in "verbal originality"—in the governing principle of "the poet's *inventio.*" Now, however, "*inventio* is giving way to appropriation, elaborate constraint, visual and sound composition, and reliance on intertextuality."[176] Bök's microbial-collaborative poetics thus must be read in terms of his approach to citation, which becomes another form of clinamen: a swerve that draws new material into the poem's ambit, a kind of lateral transfer of poetic information.

Many of the poem sequences in book 1 explore the elegiac heritage in pastoral poetry. If the Hadean setting of "The Late Heavy Bombardment" conveys a Miltonic undertone, Milton's "Lycidas" also haunts the pastoral sequences that follow. "Colony Collapse Disorder," a group of fifty blank-verse sonnets that translate book 2 of Virgil's *Georgics,* is a meditation on unintended consequences. It relates two tales of katabatic rescue: that of Aristaeus, who must enter hell to restore his collapsed hives, killed as punishment for his role in Eurydice's death, and Orpheus's failure to return Eurydice to the world. The poems depict the violent undertow of pastoral imagery ("for lizards gnaw, unseen, / into the comb") and agonize over the assumption that we can restore our own hives after so assiduously "plowing / them, like salt, into our pasture."[177] Other poems alter the notion of poetic form almost beyond recognition. "Death Sets a Thing Significant" presents four computer-generated imagery depictions of the folding sequence, atomic backbone, entire molecule, and charge envelope for a protein generated by a computer that has "misread" the title of Emily Dickinson's poem and interpreted it as a chain of amino acids. Dickinson's poem of elegiac traces, which imagines the material remnants of a departed life hailing the living, seeds Bök's ideogrammatic "poems" with doubts about the textual fixation of DNA discourse. "Now, when I read, I read not," Dickinson writes, "For interrupting tears / Obliterate the etchings."[178]

"The Nocturne of Orpheus" breaks down Keats's "When I Have Fears That I May Cease to Be" into its constituent phonemes and reassembles it as a new poem, converting the original Shakespearean sonnet into an Alexandrine blank-verse sonnet spoken by Orpheus as he waits to descend into hell. Bök's poem retains the trace of the older nocturne, however, torqueing it into a new configuration. Nocturnes, according to Susan Stewart, "bring forward the potential for seeing beyond single-point perspectives and present-centred conditions";[179] that is, they also "tend towards multiplicity" in the darkness of negative capability. "The Nocturne of Orpheus" remains haunted, like an organelle in a eukaryotic cell, by Keats's vision of mortality, in which "Love and Fame to nothingness do sink,"[180] but it simultaneously couples Keats's fears of personal annihilation with intimations of the planetary scale of what Rose calls "double death." Bök's poem is also a double acrostic, the first and last letters of each line spelling the dedication to book 1, "for the maiden in her dark pale meadow," a reference to Eurydice, who, as we shall see, stands for the quickening loss of relations in the face of the extinction crisis. Bök imposes on his poem a multidirectional reading, coupling the vertical acrostic reading (mimicking perhaps Orpheus's descent into hell) with the lateral relationship between intertexts. In doing so, he exploits not only a relationship between poems but also the latent possibilities within inherited forms.

Although neither is cited openly, Rilke's and Shakespeare's sonnet sequences haunt the Xenotext. Other kinds of traditional forms are recast according to the project's genetic exigencies. "The March of the

Nucleotides" is a pastoral sequence of three fifteen-line poems arranged to resemble the formation of a molecule of DNA. Each line consists of two words and nine letters, recalling the nine letters shared between encoding DNA sequence and the replicating RNA sequence in a codon undergoing transcription. The two words in each line are separated by a caesura, with each letter before the caesura corresponding to the nucleotide for the letter that immediately follows it (so each line may only contain words joined by *A* and *T* or *C* and *G*). In a final flourish of constraint, the caesuras align to form a zigzag, mimicking the helical shape of DNA. The three poems form a conjoined sequence: each ends with a final line that will be repeated as the first line of the ensuing poem, following an alliterative pattern. Thus the first poem opens with the line "A TREASURY" and ends with "A TAPESTRY"; the second opens with "A TAPESTRY" and becomes "A THRENODY," which, at the close of the final poem in the sequence, becomes "A TREASURY" once more—we arrive at the end with a sense of the richness of life (treasury) having first looped through tapestry and threnody, weaving a consciousness of loss into the celebration of biodiversity. As it torques its form to replicate the helical twist of DNA, "The March of the Nucleotides" also queries the celebratory rhetoric of DNA discourse in an age of extinction. The lateral shift as one reads *across* each column, from "AMASSES / VIA TWISTS" to "AFFIRMS / VIA TROPES" to "AROUSES / VIA TEMPOS," puts the emphasis on untimeliness, whereas at the foot of each column, a corresponding series, moving, for example, from "ABYSSES" to "ARCADIA" (echoing Yeats's lament "The woods of arcady are dead"), refuses to offer a consolatory resolution. The "song of life" playing through the genetic code becomes an elegy, "LONG CRIES" to "DISQUIET A / PAGEANT."[181] Rather than a hubristic celebration of the eternal poem, the Xenotext's orphic echoes moan the sorrow of the great unmaking.

Ecological elegy is, as Timothy Morton has said, future oriented. Its untimeliness, like that of the Xenotext itself, resides in the fact that it invites us to mourn that which is yet to pass.[182] Bonnie Costello has borrowed Clifton Spargo's notion of "anticipatory elegy" to describe a move she sees as characteristic of contemporary ecological elegies, to move "from mourning a particular death or extinction . . . to mourning the death of

Nature itself, as if it had already occurred."[183] This amplification of grief is nowhere more evident than in the Xenotext itself:

Orpheus	*Eurydice*
any style of life is prim	the faery is rosy of glow
oh stay my lyre	in fate we rely
with wily ploys moan the riff	moan more grief with any loss
the riff of any tune aloud	any loss is the achy trick
moan now my fate	with him we stay
in fate we rely	oh stay my lyre
my myth now is the word	we wean him of any milk
the word of life	any milk is rosy[184]

"Orpheus" seems at first to speak as the "supreme poet" of Rilke's sonnets, possessed of the "word of life." Skillman suggests that "lyre" is a metonym for genetic technology, signifying the poem's preoccupation with biogenetic processes, a reading supported by the pairing of "life" with "rosy" at the beginning and end of each poem.[185] Several critics have read in "rosy of glow" a reference to "mCherry," a red fluorescent protein that biologists often use to make transcription more visible—a self-referential nod to the poem's biochemical origins and to the fact that the bacterium does in fact glow red during transcription.[186] The couplet "in fate / we rely" carries a knowing echo of James Watson's famous, hubristic statement in support of the Human Genome Project: "We used to think our fate was in the stars, now we know it is in our genes."[187] However, the fact that the couplet repeats across both poems via the ANY-THE 112 cipher dictates that they are read not only vertically but laterally. Each poem haunts the other, implicitly present as its inverse incarnation. As if to demonstrate Bök's contention that language signifies uncannily even under the most severe restrictions, the ANY-THE 112 cipher produces a series of word pairs that echo eerily across the void. Orpheus's "riff"—the lamenting song by which he "moan[s] now my fate"—speaks, through the cipher, Eurydice's "loss"; his "wily ploys" are, for her, the precursor to "more grief." But in the midst of Eurydice's protest at Orpheus's presumption, the sense of a greater or deeper affinity underpins Bök's ecological elegies. By pairing "moan" and "with," the poems indicate that any lament over loss of life acknowledges a pregiven relationship with that life. Read laterally, the poems become an exercise in collective grieving, *moaning with* the many lost. Repetition consolidates this, as "moan the riff // the riff" becomes "with any loss // any loss"; likewise, by implication, the focus of the elegy is amplified: any (every) loss must be sung.

This is further evident in the way Bök's paired sonnets also echo with the traces of other poems. The pairing of "any style of life / is prim" and "the faery is rosy / glow" resonates with a keen sense of multispecies liveliness and frailty. Murphet traces "style of life" to *Lebensstil*, a psychiatric phrase to denote an individual's particular mode of responding to stimuli, that is, the individual's characteristic swerve toward or away from the world, the apostrophe that constitutes his particular "linguistic being."[188] As this phrase translates into its counterpart in "Eurydice," it sets off a chain of associations that culminate in a howl of grief at the loss of a world of relations.

Beyond fluorescing mCherry, "rosy" invokes Yeats's use of the rose as a sorrowing symbol of eternal beauty ("far-off, most secret and inviolate rose," "beauty grown sad with its eternity").[189] If, as Skillman argues, this allusion "reanimates Romantic analogies between divine creation and *poiesis*"[190] (a reading supported by Bök's references to Keats throughout book 1), then we need to take account of where such an allusion leads. Yeats's insistence on the generative potential in the fairy was bound to a vision of "a world where anything might flow and change, and become any other thing,"[191] that is, by a notion of lively interchange and transformation, a symbiotic vision at odds with the vertical integration of gene fetishism. Yeats's ideas were significantly influenced by William Blake, for whom the "imaginative arts" were akin to "sympathy with all living things."[192] The Blake that so shaped Yeats's thinking also haunts the rosy glow in "Eurydice," investing the poem with a kin-making sensibility. But with Blake, the poem swerves again; the most famous rose in Blake is the sick rose, plagued by an "invisible worm" whose "dark secret love / Does thy life destroy."[193] Through Bök's "Eurydice," the bacterium protests at the "achy trick" imposed upon it. The resilience of *D. radiodurans* suggests this ought not be read literally but, again, laterally—from the particular to the general, protesting also against the wider regimes of violence that are driving extinction. Haunting the celebration of biogenetic potential, then, is a far darker acknowledgment of the violence that inheres in such projects and in multispecies relations generally.

"Orpheus" and "Eurydice" present a pair of voices that clash with, contest, and speak in opposition to one another. The repeated phrases "oh stay / my lyre" and "in fate / we rely" occur in both poems, but inverted, so that the apostrophe of Orpheus belongs, in the end, to Eurydice. Conventionally, Eurydice is herself no more than a cipher. Maurice Blanchot calls her "the limit of what art can attain."[194] But Bök's defiant "Eurydice" is closer to the raging figure in H.D.'s poem of the same name, who berates Orpheus for his thoughtless arrogance while defiantly declaring her own self-defining presence. Whereas Orpheus solipsistically laments himself in the loss of Eurydice, her lament is for the loss of the lively world of kin-making, where "all the flowers are lost."[195] Before she is lost forever, she warns, "hell must open *like a red rose* / for the dead to pass."[196] "Eurydice" is reimagined by both H.D. and Bök as a howl of protest at the rupture of "double death." The Xenotext is thus an expression of "anticipatory mourning."[197] As the "eternal poem" inclines toward the very deep future, it does so keenly alert to the prospect of how deeply impoverished that future may be. Ecological elegy, as Morton puts it, "asks us to mourn for something that has not yet completely passed."[198] Thus the Xenotext sings of a future haunting; but, as Avery Gordon has said, haunting is also "a demand for a liveable future."[199] In voicing his protest at the great unmaking of the world through Eurydice, whose name means something like "wide justice," Bök implicitly insists that we turn away from the course upon which we are set.

A poetics of kin-making starts with the dynamic of life itself: its capacity to swerve toward relation, its collaborative impulse. Knottedness does not only signify the braiding of individual lives, however. It also implies the entanglement of flight ways. As we swerve toward or away from the creatures with whom we share coevolutionary histories, we reach into deep time, either deepening connections or severing them. As van Dooren says, to meet any particular animal is also to witness the *times* that animal "ties together" along its flight way: "not 'the past' and 'the future' as abstract temporal horizons, but real embodied generations—ancestors and descendants—in rich but imperfect relationships of inheritance, nourishment, and care."[200] In a time of extinction, these creaturely encounters are increasingly haunted by the prospect of ruptured flight ways drawn to a premature close.

The animal others encountered in this chapter possess a spectral presence; each one is both itself and the harbinger of a future haunting. Doty's jellyfish, whose physical form is most obviously ghostly, recedes eerily from view even as the poem fills with its likeness. The parade of cnidarian doppelgangers (heart, balloon, parasol) evokes the human waste that is filling the oceans, altering its ecology and contributing to the conditions for increasing jellyfish blooms at the expense of most other marine life. Doty's poem shows the difficulty of inclining in language toward the nonhuman, as both language and the animal torque and swerve away from any final "capture." Instead, the poem multiplies the number of times inhabited by the poem, invoking a possible deep future of desertified oceans, a Precambrian return teeming with cnidarian life and little else. Borodale's bees, similarly, withdraw from the poet's attention. But his persistence in writing at the hive, cultivating intimacy through proximity and patience, dilutes his sense of himself. The strain placed on the lyric "I" in *Bee Journal* figures the beekeeper as a ghostly presence, increasingly insubstantial to himself in contrast with the lively materiality of the colony. The collapse into elegy when the hive dies presages a much greater dying, one that is itself already taking place.

Both Doty and Borodale are haunted by futures of ecological collapse; in response to this, they incline toward collaboration with their animal subjects. The title of Doty's poem "Difference" indicates his intention to write against the vision of a homogenized future biome, even as the poem forcefully foreshadows this. He adopts the jellyfish's materiality, its insuperable difference, as the vehicle for the poem; counterintuitively, the basis for Doty's effort to multiply the bonds of kin-making with jellyfish is their profound resistance to becoming kin. Borodale's clinamen involves a surrender of poetic privilege, relinquishing the capacity to determine the subject or occasion of the poem to the priorities of the hive. *Bee Journal* represents a multispecies collaborative poetics, a jointly authored work with millions of contributors. As such, it is a compelling portrait of the knottedness of our being with others, even as that knottedness is denied, exploited, and neglected.

These themes of spectral futures and multispecies collaboration come together with remarkable synergy in Christian Bök's Xenotext experiment. Bök's endeavor to collaborate with an undying microbe, as the basis for an ecological elegy that will (if the project is successful) sound into the unimaginably deep future, is a compelling reflection both on environmental hubris and the lively swerve of life toward life. If, as Doty and Borodale also infer, language is our primary means of kin-making (however flawed), Bök shows how we can discover connection, the furtherance of life and meaning, in the most constrained circumstances. Metamorphosing through a series of radically different forms and scales (cryptographic, digital, proteomic), the Xenotext illustrates the uncanny resilience of language as well as life. Bök's reliance on, even revelry in, textual metaphors could therefore be seen as a necessary hubris. In making kin, we cannot kid ourselves; becoming with others is not a swerve away from the things that mark us out as human but a deepening of these very differences. It is especially significant that Haraway's list of tentacular creatures includes "fingery beings," embedding the human in a web of associations that is wholly unfamiliar yet also, somehow, determines something of what being human is about—"fingeryness" connoting tool making and ingenuity, a capacity to shape and mold environments. Following an encounter with the animal other, we return to ourselves newly alert to our own strangeness. In light of this, the great irony of the Xenotext—that the vehicle and coauthor of the lament for the breaking of the world of relations is itself unbreakable—is its most significant clinamen. Willfully "misreading" extinction in this way, via a life-form that is "extinction proof," allows Bök to incline toward an unimaginably distant deep future, to discover community and creativity in the haunting presence of species death.

Supertrees, Singapore, 2017. Photograph by David Farrier.

Coda

KNOTS IN TIME

It is the end of January, and I am standing on a narrow walkway twenty-two meters above the ground, in the canopy of a grove of trees unlike any I have ever seen before. The tallest is fifty meters high. Their vine-wrapped metal trunks are topped by large solar panels, although I can't see them glinting in the sunlight for the fractal maze of thin, magenta branches, more like roots on an inverted tree, sprouting crazily from the tops of the columnar boles. From here, the view is arresting. I can see the rest of the fantastical grove curving away in an elegant arc, above the colorful, teeming splendor of Singapore's botanical gardens. Beyond, an archipelago of container ships floats benignly in the bay, forests of cranes on the shore ready to relieve them of their burdens. Behind me, a glittering escarpment of glass and steel high-rise buildings marks the financial district, one of the wealthiest in the world; $1.2 trillion flowed through it in 2016 alone.

Singapore's "supertrees" seem like the harbingers of an already outdated future, like the utopian imaginings of 1960s science fiction made real. They are the emblems of the Garden City as it would like to be seen in the twenty-first century. In fact, the supertrees are an ingenious combination of giant solar panels and vents for the heat generated from creating electricity from the city's waste biomass. In this respect, they exemplify the notion that technology will offer a way out of the ecological corner into which we have painted ourselves. And yet standing in the artificial canopy seems to be an encounter with a rather different kind of Anthropocenic moment.

It is a moment thickened by the collision of countless species' flight ways and intra-acting "stories that matter." The gardens were founded on fifty-four hectares of land reclaimed from the sea. Despite Singapore's pastoral pretensions (greenery is everywhere, even decorating the sides of office and apartment buildings), it is one of the most urbanized places on the planet—87 percent of the shoreline is coated in concrete, creating a near-complete stone collar around the island.[1] A sign on the walkway encourages visitors to look for the garden's highest flowering orchid, blown onto the platform by the wind. Singapore is famous for its native orchids, but the garden is also filled with imported species (many housed inside two enormous climate-controlled greenhouses, one of which exhibits a gallery of ecosystems from across the globe, the other of which replicates a cloud forest, complete with indoor mountain and waterfall), echoing the rise in invasive species across the island (a colonial legacy, exacerbated by Singapore's position as a hub for global shipping). Information boards at the base of the supertrees explain the impact of deforestation on the soil cycle and how a process of replenishment that takes only twenty-four hours in a tropical rainforest environment can become instead locked into millennial cycles of sedimentation and erosion if the nutrient-rich soils are washed away into the ocean.

Different expressions of human-inflected deep time flow through the scene: in the panoply of products entombed in the containers, in the patina of carbon residue from the forest fires in neighboring Borneo that might find its way into an ice core thousands of miles away, or in the soundless crashing of tropical biodiversity. The skies are clear, but in recent years, for much of June through October, the island has been enveloped in a thick smog blown in from illegal and uncontrolled fires, used to clear Indonesian rain forests and make way for giant palm oil plantations. The Garden City is a node in a vast network of extraction and consumption, linked to countless shadow places across the planet where the container-ized goods originate and which the financial district (itself a kind of shadow place garlanded in flowers) monetizes. It is a place in which kin-making is subsumed by commodification.

The largest supertree contains an exhibition on climate change. Beginning at the top, visitors are walked through the science on a katabatic journey into the very worst possible effects of uncontrolled emissions. A video projected on a giant screen on the lowest level itemizes the cost of each fractional rise in global temperatures: at +1.8 degrees, all coral reefs are bleached; at +2.9 degrees, half of all species are set on a fixed course to extinction; at 4.3 degrees, the amount of available freshwater halves. Finally, the voice-over intones, at 5 degrees above preindustrial levels by 2100, "the earth is a dry rock dying in space."

Standing on the walkway is like entering a knot in time. Deborah Bird Rose counsels that we are, all of us, "dense knots of embodied time," braided from uncountable strands of cross-species actions and giftings.[2] A poem is also knot in time, a complex of matter and sensation and memory. It can both stretch and compress a moment of perception to reveal the flux of scales that enfold us in deep time. It can reveal the uneven grain beneath the apparently smooth surface of the world. It can conjure figures that concretize the Anthropocene's provocations to what we imagine our future to hold. What I have tried to show in *Anthropocene Poetics* is how poetry can give shape and form to the density of this knottedness.

In Elizabeth Bishop's lyric plays on continuity, change, and scale, and in Seamus Heaney's time-thickened verse, open to the intrusion of other times and places in the given moment, we encounter the capacity of lyric poetry to draw vastly distant temporalities within the compass of intimate experience. Just as the Anthropocene is a challenge to what makes us human, Bishop's and Heaney's work shows us that geologic intimacy is a condition of being human. We are shaped biologically, socially, and culturally by our mineral inheritance, as Povinelli, Yusoff, and Clark insist. Reading poetry that conveys this sense of geologic intimacy helps to set the parameters for an Anthropocene poetics. In a fashion, Bishop and Heaney beat the bounds of the territory explored in the work of the other poets featured in this study. Peter Larkin's discovery of plenitude in what he calls the "thrive-margin"[3] of plantation spaces, an archetypal shadow place or sacrifice zone, and Evelyn Reilly's vigorous portrayal of the liveliness of seemingly inert materials like Styrofoam show how this enfolding with deep time also implicates us in relations of violence. Where, in Bishop and Heaney, lyric poetry draws us into a complex of sensual engagements with deep time, Larkin's and Reilly's open field excursions disturb notions of disposability and return a sense of story to sites and materials denuded of history by extractivist practices. Mark Doty, Sean Borodale, and Christian Bök address the unpicking of these knots, what Rose calls the "great unmaking."[4] Through the figure of the clinamen, their work urges us to swerve back toward life and to see that our responsibility in the Anthropocene is to cultivate collaborative rather than exploitative relations with other species. It reminds us that life is an ongoing process of multispecies *poiesis,* a perpetual mutual making.

"Poetry makes nothing happen"—so warned W. H. Auden in his elegy for W. B. Yeats.[5] Neither do I want to overstate the case for poetry in the Anthropocene. However, an Anthropocene poetics—of relations thickened in deep time, of our entanglement with sacrifice zones, and of the inexorable drive of kin-making—can help frame the ground we stand on as we consider which way to turn. As Heaney wrote, we can, if we choose, dismiss the efficacy of poetry out of hand. And yet, if we allow it, it offers "a break with the usual life, but not an absconding from it." Poetry, he says,

> marks time in every possible sense of that phrase. It does not . . . propose to be instrumental or effective. Instead, in the rift between what is going to happen and whatever we would wish to happen, poetry holds attention for a space, functions not as distraction but as pure concentration, a focus where our power to concentrate is concentrated back on ourselves.[6]

This rift is like the Anthropocenic moment, the knot in time, not because it creates a solipsism but because, in focusing attention back on *us,* it asks the question, what will you do? A poetics of the Anthropocene must occupy this rift. In doing so, it can point us toward a careful retying of the knots that bind us together, in deep time, with the fate of the Earth.

Notes

INTRODUCTION

1 Jessica Mairs, "Alex Chinneck Unveils Installation Modelled on Upside-Down Electricity Pylon," *dezeen,* September 15, 2015, https://www.dezeen.com/.

2 Crutzen, a Nobel Prize–winning atmospheric chemist, was not the first to refer to the Anthropocene, a fact acknowledged in his coauthorship, with Eugene Stoermer, of the paper that popularized the term. Stoermer had used it informally since the 1980s, and a U.S. journalist, Andrew Revkin, had proposed the "Anthrocene" in 1992. Before them all, an Italian geologist called Antonio Stoppani coined the term "Anthropozoic Era," cited by George Perkins Marsh in 1873, only forty years after the first use of "Holocene" by Charles Lyell in 1833. However, Crutzen's outburst at a conference in Mexico City at the turn of the millennium, which has since assumed a kind of mythic status, marked its entry into discourse—not a true origin, then, but the point when an idea finally acquired the momentum to carry it into public consciousness. See Paul Crutzen and Eugene Stoermer, "The 'Anthropocene,'" *Global Change Newsletter* 41 (2000): 17–18; Will Steffen, Jacques Grinevald, Paul Crutzen, and John McNeill, "The Anthropocene: Conceptual and Historical Perspectives," *Philosophical Transactions of the Royal Society, Series A* 369 (2011): 842–67.

3 Clive Hamilton, "The Anthropocene as Rupture," *The Anthropocene Review* 3, no. 2 (2016): 97.

4 Clive Hamilton, "Getting the Anthropocene So Wrong," *The Anthropocene Review* 2, no. 2 (2015): 102–7.

5 Mark A. Maslin and Simon L. Lewis, "Anthropocene: Earth System, Geological, Philosophical and Political Paradigm Shift," *The Anthropocene Review* 2, no. 2 (2015): 114.

6 Jan Zalasiewicz, "The Extraordinary Strata of the Anthropocene," in *Environmental Humanities: Voices from the Anthropocene,* ed. Serpil

Oppermann and Serenella Iovino (London: Rowman and Littlefield, 2017), 124.

7 William Rueckert, "Literature and Ecology: An Experiment in Eco-criticism," in *The Ecocriticism Reader,* ed. Cheryll Glotfelty and Harold Fromm (Athens: University of Georgia Press, 1996), 105–23.

8 Lawrence Buell, *The Environmental Imagination: Thoreau, Nature Writing, and the Formation of American Culture* (Cambridge, Mass.: Harvard University Press, 1995), 7.

9 Timothy Clark, *Ecocriticism at the Edge: The Anthropocene as a Threshold Concept* (London: Bloomsbury, 2015), 19.

10 Robert Macfarlane, *Landmarks* (Hamish Hamilton, 2015), 27.

11 Rueckert, "Literature and Ecology," 108.

12 Jonathan Culler, *Theory of the Lyric* (Cambridge, Mass.: Harvard University Press, 2015), 294.

13 Matthew Griffiths, *The New Poetics of Climate Change* (London: Bloomsbury, 2017), 10.

14 Griffiths, 19.

15 Michelle Bastian, "Fatally Confused: Telling the Time in the Midst of Ecological Crises," *Journal of Environmental Philosophy* 9, no. 1 (2012): 23–48.

16 Michelle Bastian and Thom van Dooren, "The New Immortals: Immortality and Infinitude in the Anthropocene," *Environmental Philosophy* 14, no. 1 (2017): 1.

17 Bastian and van Dooren, 5.

18 Ben Dibley, "'The Shape of Things to Come': Seven Theses on the Anthropocene and Attachment," *Australian Humanities Review* 52 (2012), http://australianhumanitiesreview.org/.

19 Tom Bristow, *The Anthropocene Lyric: An Affective Geography of Poetry, Person, and Place* (London: Palgrave, 2015).

20 Sam Solnick, *Poetry and the Anthropocene: Ecology, Biology, and Technology in Contemporary British and Irish Poetry* (London: Routledge, 2016), 4.

21 Simon Dalby, "Framing the Anthropocene: The Good, the Bad, and the Ugly," *The Anthropocene Review* 3, no. 1 (2016): 33–51.

22 Jason W. Moore, *Capitalism in the Web of Life: Ecology and the Accumulation of Capital* (London: Verso, 2015).

23 Andreas Malm and Alf Hornborg, "The Geology of Mankind? A Critique of the Anthropocene Narrative," *The Anthropocene Review* 1, no. 1 (2014): 65.

24 Eileen Crist, "On the Poverty of Our Nomenclature," *Environmental Humanities* 3 (2013): 136.

25 Daniel Cunha, "The Geology of the Ruling Class?," *The Anthropocene Review* 2, no. 3 (2015): 263, 264.

26 Evelyn Reilly, "Eco-noise and the Flux of Lux," in *)((eco(lang) (uage (reader))*, ed. Brenda Iijima (New York: Portable Press/Nightboat Books, 2010), 258.

27 Dipesh Chakrabarty, "The Climate of History: Four Theses," *Critical Inquiry* 35, no. 2 (2009): 206.

28 John Playfair, *The Works of John Playfair* (Edinburgh: Archibald, Constable, 1822), 4:80.

29 Kathryn Yusoff, "Geologic Life: Prehistory, Climate, Futures in the Anthropocene," *Environment and Planning D: Society and Space* 31 (2013): 779.

30 Yusoff, 785.

31 Moore, *Capitalism in the Web of Life*, 44.

32 Timothy Morton, *Hyperobjects: Philosophy and Ecology after the End of the World* (Minneapolis: University of Minnesota Press, 2013).

33 Peter Larkin, "Fully From, All Scarce To," in Iijima, *)((eco(lang) (uage (reader))*, 55.

34 Val Plumwood, "Shadow Places and the Politics of Dwelling," *Australian Humanities Review* 44 (2008), http://www.australianhumanitiesreview .org/; Naomi Klein, *This Changes Everything: Capitalism vs the Climate* (London: Allen Lane, 2014), 172, 222.

35 Larkin, "Fully From, All Scarce To," 52, 55.

36 Evelyn Reilly, "Eco-noise and the Flux of Lux," 258.

37 Reilly, 261.

38 Thom van Dooren, *Flight Ways: Life and Loss at the Edge of Extinction* (London: Columbia University Press, 2014), 27.

39 Deborah Bird Rose, "Multispecies Knots of Ethical Time," *Environmental Philosophy* 9, no. 1 (2012): 127–40.

40 van Dooren, *Flight Ways*, 27–29.

1. INTIMACY

1 Ilana Halperin, "Physical Geology (a Field Guide to New Landmass in Three Formations)," in *Ilana Halperin: New Landmass/Neue Landmasse*, ed. Sara Barnes and Andrew Patrizio (Berlin: Berliner Medizinhisto-rischen Museum der Charité/Shering Stiftung, 2012), 52.

2 Jan Zalasiewicz, Mark Williams, and Colin N. Waters, "The Technofossil Record of Humans," *The Anthropocene Review* 1, no. 1 (2014): 34–43.

3 Dipesh Chakrabarty, "The Climate of History: Four Theses," *Critical Inquiry* 35, no. 2 (2009): 206.

4 Eileen Crist, "On the Poverty of Our Nomenclature," *Environmental Humanities* 3 (2013): 141.

5 Jan Zalasiewicz, "The Extraordinary Strata of the Anthropocene," in *Environmental Humanities: Voices from the Anthropocene,* ed. Serpil Oppermann and Serenella Iovino (London: Rowman and Littlefield, 2017), 124; Elizabeth A. Povinelli, *Geontologies: A Requiem to Late Liberalism* (Durham, N.C.: Duke University Press, 2016), 13.

6 Kathryn Yusoff, "Geologic Life: Prehistory, Climate, Futures in the Anthropocene," *Environment and Planning D: Society and Space* 31 (2013): 781.

7 Bruno Latour, *We Have Never Been Modern,* trans. Catherine Porter (Cambridge, Mass.: Harvard University Press, 1991); Jane Bennett, *Vibrant Matter: A Political Ecology of Things* (Durham, N.C.: Duke University Press, 2010); Quentin Meillassoux, *After Finitude,* trans. Ray Brassier (New York: Continuum, 2008).

8 Gísli Pálsson and Heather A. Swanson, "Down to Earth: Geosocialities and Geopolitics," *Environmental Humanities* 8, no. 2 (2016): 155.

9 Ilana Halperin, "Autobiographical Trace Fossils," in *Making the Geologic Now: Responses to Material Conditions of Contemporary Life,* ed. Elizabeth Ellsworth and Jamie Kruse (Brooklyn, N.Y.: Punctum Books, 2013), 156.

10 Halperin, 158.

11 Halperin, "Physical Geology," 52.

12 Elizabeth Ellsworth and Jamie Kruse, "Evidence: Making a Geologic Turn in Cultural Awareness," in Ellsworth and Kruse, *Making the Geologic Now,* 23.

13 Jeffrey Jerome Cohen, *Stone: An Ecology of the Inhuman* (Minneapolis: University of Minnesota Press, 2015), 14.

14 Cohen, 43.

15 Cohen, 23–24.

16 Timothy Morton, "Queer Ecology," *PMLA* 125, no. 2 (2010): 274.

17 Astrida Neimanis and Rachel Loewen Walker, "Weathering: Climate Change and the 'Thick Time' of Transcorporeality," *Hypatia* 29, no. 3 (2014): 561; Astrida Neimanis, Cecilia Åsberg, and Johan Hedrén, "Four Problems, Four Directions: Toward a Critical Posthumanities for the Anthropocene," *Ethics and the Environment* 20, no. 1 (2015): 69.

18 Deborah Bird Rose, *Wild Dog Dreaming: Love and Extinction* (Charlottesville: University of Virginia Press, 2011), 12.

19 Jonathan Culler, *Theory of the Lyric* (Cambridge, Mass.: Harvard University Press, 2015), 226, 294.

20 Mary Kinzie, *The Cure of Poetry in an Age of Prose* (Chicago: University of Chicago Press, 1993), 210.

21 Pálsson and Swanson, "Down to Earth," 153.

22 Stephanie LeMenager, *Living Oil: Petroleum Cultures in the American Century* (Oxford: Oxford University Press, 2015), 69.

23 Mimi Sheller and John Urry, "The City and the Car," *International Journal of Urban and Regional Research* 24, no. 4 (2000): 739.

24 Cohen, *Stone*, 14.

25 Timothy Clark, "Derangements of Scale," in *Telemorphosis: Theory in an Era of Climate Change,* ed. Tom Cohen (London: Open Humanities Press, 2012), 1:152.

26 Clark, 153.

27 Michel Foucault, *The Order of Things* (1970; repr., New York: Random House, 1994), xvii.

28 Jorge Luis Borges, *The Aleph and Other Stories, 1933–1969* (London: Penguin, 2000), 130.

29 Borges, 131, 130.

30 Clark, "Derangements," 153.

31 Bernd M. Scherer, preface to *Textures of the Anthropocene: Grain, Vapor, Ray—Manual,* ed. Katrin Klingan, Ashkan Sepahvand, Christoph Rosol, and Bernd M. Scherer (Cambridge, Mass.: MIT Press, 2014), 20.

32 Morton, "Queer Ecology," 274.

33 Anne Colwell, *Inscrutable Houses: Metaphors of the Body in the Poems of Elizabeth Bishop* (Tuscaloosa: University of Alabama Press, 1997), 197; Susan McCabe, *Elizabeth Bishop: Her Poetics of Loss* (University Park: Pennsylvania State University Press, 1994), xii.

34 Victoria Harrison, *Elizabeth Bishop's Poetics of Intimacy* (Cambridge: Cambridge University Press, 1993), 11, 17.

35 Linda Anderson, *Elizabeth Bishop: Lines of Connection* (Edinburgh: Edinburgh University Press, 2013), 3.

36 Harrison, *Elizabeth Bishop's Poetics of Intimacy,* 9.

37 Susannah L. Hollister, "Elizabeth Bishop's Geographic Feeling," *Twentieth-Century Literature* 58, no. 3 (2012): 399.

38 Bonnie Costello, *Elizabeth Bishop: Questions of Mastery* (Cambridge, Mass.: Harvard University Press, 1991), 118.

39 Elizabeth Bishop, *Poems: The Centenary Edition* (London: Chatto and Windus, 2011), 91.

40 Bishop, 65, 66.

41 Bishop, 82.

42 Seamus Heaney, *Finders Keepers: Selected Prose 1971–2001* (London: Faber, 2002), 339, 340.

43 Hollister, "Elizabeth Bishop's Geographic Feeling," 422.

44 Bishop, *Poems,* 129.

45 Susan Stewart, *On Longing: Narratives of the Miniature, the Gigantic, the Souvenir and the Collection* (Baltimore: The Johns Hopkins University Press, 1984), 65, 67.

46 Klingan et al., *Textures of the Anthropocene,* 7.

47 McCabe, *Poetics of Loss,* 14.

48 Elizabeth Grosz, *Time Travels: Feminism, Nature, Power* (Durham, N.C.: Duke University Press, 2005), 3.

49 Hollister, "Elizabeth Bishop's Geographic Feeling," 410.

50 Cohen, *Stone,* 23.

51 Bishop, *Poems,* 5.

52 Elizabeth Grosz, "Becoming . . . an Introduction," in *Becomings: Explorations in Time, Memory, and Futures,* ed. Elizabeth Grosz (Ithaca, N.Y.: Cornell University Press, 1999), 3–4.

53 Bishop, as quoted in Colwell, *Inscrutable Houses,* 192.

54 Elizabeth Bishop, as quoted in Anderson, *Elizabeth Bishop,* 4.

55 Bishop, as quoted in Anderson, 46, italics original.

56 Harrison, *Elizabeth Bishop's Poetics of Intimacy,* 37.

57 Zachariah Pickard, "Natural History and Epiphany: Elizabeth Bishop's Darwin Letter," *Twentieth Century* 50, no. 3 (2004): 269.

58 Charles Darwin, *The Origin of Species* (1869; repr., Harmondsworth, U.K.: Penguin, 1975), 65, 72.

59 Darwin, *Origin,* 114, 115.

60 Bishop, *Poems,* 62.

61 Darwin, *Origin,* 107.

62 Louis MacNeice, *Selected Poems* (London: Faber, 1988), 23.

63 Morton, "Queer Ecology," 275.

64 Timothy Morton, "Ecology as Text, Text as Ecology," *Oxford Literary Review* 32, no. 1 (2010): 2.

65 Grosz, *Time Travels,* 21.

66 Timothy Morton, "The Mesh," in *Environmental Criticism in the Twenty-First Century,* ed. Stephanie LeMenager, Teresa Shewry, and Ken Hiltner (London: Routledge, 2011), 20.

67 Morton, 64.

68 Cohen, *Stone,* 20.
69 Morton, "Queer Ecology," 275.
70 Yusoff, "Geologic Life," 780.
71 Nigel Clark, *Inhuman Nature: Social Life on a Dynamic Planet* (London: Sage, 2011), 52.
72 Fiona S. Tweed, "Now That the Dust Has Settled . . . ," *Geology Today* 28, no. 6 (2012): 217.
73 Bishop, *Poems,* 185.
74 Costello, *Elizabeth Bishop,* 203.
75 Bishop, *Poems,* 183.
76 Bishop, 185.
77 Costello, *Elizabeth Bishop,* 118.
78 Bishop, *Poems,* 180.
79 Hollister, "Geographic Feeling," 425.
80 Timothy Clark, *Ecocriticism on the Edge* (London: Bloomsbury, 2015), 33.
81 Timothy Luke, "On Environmentality: Geo-Power and Eco-Knowledge in the Discourses of Contemporary Environmentalism," *Cultural Critique* 31 (1995): 64.
82 Lee Edelman, "The Geography of Gender: Elizabeth Bishop's 'In the Waiting Room,'" *Contemporary Literature* 26, no. 2 (1985): 188.
83 Bishop, *Poems,* 185.
84 Morton, "Queer Ecology," 275.
85 Myra J. Hird, *The Origins of Sociable Life: Evolution after Science Studies* (Basingstoke, U.K.: Palgrave Macmillan, 2009), 22, 51, 26. If ecological science has come to understand the human body as an ecosystem, it is a profoundly odd, even unsettling one composed of multiple different expressions of deep time. Viruses possess their own deep time: viral evolution occurs over generations that can last as little as twenty-four hours, permitting tens of thousands of iterations that virologists are able to observe in laboratory conditions—literally, watching evolution unfold before their eyes. This "fast" deep time or viral deep time is an essential component of who we are. Elizabeth Costello et al., "The Application of Ecological Theory toward an Understanding of the Human Microbiome," *Science* 336 (2012): 125-26; Robert J. Gifford, "Viral Evolution in Deep Time: Lentiviruses and Mammals," *Trends in Genetics* 28, no. 2 (2012): 89-100; Richard E. Lenski, "Evolution in Action: A 50,000 Generation Salute to Charles Darwin," *Microbe* 6, no. 1 (2011): 30-33.
86 Grosz, *Time Travels,* 145.

87 Edelman, "Geography of Gender," 188.
88 Sara Barnes and Andrew Patrizio, "A Curatorial Point in Time: *Hand Held Lava* and *Steine*," in Barnes and Patrizio, *Ilana Halperin*, 18.
89 Heaney, *Finders Keepers*, 366.
90 Seamus Heaney, *Preoccupations: Selected Prose 1968–1978* (London: Faber, 1980), 56.
91 Helen Vendler, *Seamus Heaney* (London: Fontana Press, 1998), 2.
92 Susanna Lindström and Greg Garrard, "'Images Adequate to Our Predicament': Ecology, Environment, and Ecopoetics," *Environmental Humanities* 5 (2014): 43.
93 Heaney, *Preoccupations*, 19.
94 Seamus Heaney, *Human Chain* (London: Faber, 2010), 34.
95 Heaney, *Preoccupations*, 129.
96 Seamus Heaney, *The Redress of Poetry* (Oxford: Clarendon Press, 1990), 180.
97 Heaney, *Human Chain*, 34.
98 Seamus Heaney, *Seeing Things* (London: Faber, 1991), 55.
99 Manuel DeLanda, "The Geology of Morals—A Neomaterialist Interpretation," http://future-nonstop.org/.
100 Helen Vendler, *Seamus Heaney* (London: Fontana, 1999), 142.
101 Seamus Heaney, in Denis O'Driscoll, *Stepping Stones: Interviews with Seamus Heaney* (London: Faber, 2008), 156.
102 Heaney, *Redress of Poetry*, 2.
103 Seamus Heaney, *North* (London: Faber, 1975), 13.
104 Heaney, 23.
105 Heaney, 13, 14
106 Seamus Heaney, *Death of a Naturalist* (London: Faber, 1966), 21, 22; Seamus Heaney, *The Haw Lantern* (London: Faber, 1987), 1.
107 Heaney, *Seeing Things*, 69.
108 Heaney, *North*, 14.
109 Graham Harman, "Asymmetrical Causation: Influence without Recompense," *Parallax* 16, no. 1 (2010): 100. This is seen too, perhaps, in Crusoe's reflections on the knife on his shelf in "Crusoe in England," which once "reeked of meaning" but now from which "the living soul has dribbled away." Bishop, *Poems*, 186.
110 Heaney, *Seeing Things*, 78, 65.
111 Heaney, 46.
112 Seamus Heaney, *District and Circle* (London: Faber, 2006), 5.
113 Heaney, *Seeing Things*, 17
114 Bennett, *Vibrant Matter*, 61.

115 Meillassoux, *After Finitude,* 10.
116 Povinelli, *Geontologies,* 75.
117 Povinelli, 75.
118 Povinelli, 75.
119 Seamus Heaney, *New Selected Poems 1966–1987* (London: Faber, 1990), 150.
120 Heaney, *Haw Lantern,* 37.
121 Yusoff, "Geologic Life," 788.
122 Heaney, *Finders Keepers,* 58.
123 Heaney, *Seeing Things,* 50.
124 Seamus Heaney, *Field Work* (London: Faber, 1979), 39.
125 Heaney, *Seeing Things,* 55, 56.
126 Vendler, *Seamus Heaney,* 137, 145.
127 Clark, "Geo-politics and the Disaster of the Anthropocene," *The Sociological Review* 62 (2014): 27–28.
128 Clark, 27–28.
129 Heaney, *Seeing Things,* 64.
130 Alfred Tennyson, *In Memoriam: A Norton Critical Edition,* ed. Erik Gray (New York: W. W. Norton, 2004), 92; Heaney, *New Selected Poems,* 151.
131 Alice Oswald, *Woods, Etc.* (London: Faber, 2005), 21.
132 Tim Robinson, *Stones of Aran: Pilgrimage* (London: Faber, 2008), 46.
133 W. H. Auden, *Collected Shorter Poems 1927–1957* (London: Faber, 1966), 238, 239, 240; Edna Longley, *Poetry and Posterity* (Northumberland, U.K.: Bloodaxe Books, 2000), 170, 175.
134 Yusoff, "Geologic Life," 780.
135 Kathryn Yusoff, "Geologic Subjects: Nonhuman Origins, Geomorphic Aesthetics and the Art of Becoming Inhuman," *Cultural Geographies* 22, no. 3 (2015): 384.
136 Yusoff, 386.
137 Yusoff, 389; see Rosalyn Diprose, *Corporeal Generosity: On Giving with Nietzsche, Merleau-Ponty, and Levinas* (Albany: State University of New York Press, 2002).
138 Heaney, *New and Selected Poems,* 209.
139 Yusoff, "Geologic Subjects," 18.
140 See Nigel Thrift, "Driving in the City," *Theory, Culture, and Society* 21, no. 4/5 (2004): 41–59.
141 Jack Katz, *How Emotions Work* (Chicago: University of Chicago Press, 2000), 32.
142 Heaney, *New and Selected Poems,* 207.
143 Seamus Heaney, *The Spirit Level* (London: Faber, 1996), 70.

144 Jonathan Bate, *The Song of the Earth* (London: Picador, 2000), 203.

145 Heaney, *Spirit Level,* 70.

146 Heaney, *New and Selected Poems,* 11.

147 Seamus Heaney, *Electric Light* (London: Faber, 2001), 26.

148 LeMenager, *Living Oil,* 104.

149 Mimi Sheller, "Automotive Emotions: Feeling the Car," *Theory, Culture, and Society* 21, no. 4/5 (2004): 227.

150 Sheller and Urry, "City and the Car," 738.

151 Jan Zalasiewicz, "A History in Layers," *Scientific American* 315, no. 3 (2016), https://www.scientificamerican.com/.

152 Heaney, *Field Work,* 11.

153 Rebecca Stott, *Oysters* (London: Reaktion Books, 2004), 13.

154 Stott, 31.

155 LeMenager, *Living Oil,* 69.

156 Yusoff, "Geologic Life," 788.

157 Timothy Morton, *Hyperobjects: Philosophy and Ecology after the End of the World* (Minneapolis: University of Minnesota Press, 2013), 15.

158 Morton, 1. While the striking range of Morton's examples illustrates his assertion that the hyperobject operates at multiple scales, it must be noted that he runs the risk of smoothing over both the crucial differences between and the relations within his examples. This principle of nondifferentiation occludes, for instance, that it is the capitalist world-ecology that makes Lago Agrio into an oil field.

159 Morton, 27, 64.

160 Heaney, *New and Selected Poems,* 5.

2. ENTANGLED

1 Kathleen Jamie, *Findings* (London: Sort Of Books, 2005), 59.

2 Jamie, 60.

3 Kathleen Jamie, interview in *Scotsman,* April 14, 2012.

4 Val Plumwood, "Shadow Places and the Politics of Dwelling," *Australian Humanities Review* 44 (2008), http://www.australianhumanitiesreview.org/.

5 Naomi Klein, "Let Them Drown: The Violence of Othering in a Warming World," *London Review of Books* 38, no. 11 (2016): 12; see also Naomi Klein, *This Changes Everything: Capitalism vs the Climate* (London: Allen Lane, 2014), 172, 222.

6 Jason W. Moore, *Capitalism in the Web of Life: Ecology and the Accumulation of Capital* (London: Verso, 2015), 2.

7 Jacques Rancière, *The Politics of Aesthetics,* trans. Gabriel Rockhill (London: Continuum, 2004).

8 Moore, *Capitalism in the Web of Life,* 7.

9 See https://littoralartproject.com/.

10 Anna Tsing, "On Nonscalability: The Living World Is Not Amenable to Precision-Nested Scales," *Common Knowledge* 18, no. 3 (2012): 507, 505.

11 Anna Tsing, *The Mushroom at the End of the World: On the Possibility of Life in Capitalist Ruins* (Princeton, N.J.: Princeton University Press, 2015), 6.

12 Karen Barad, *Meeting the Universe Halfway: Quantum Physics and the Entanglement of Matter and Meaning* (Durham, N.C.: Duke University Press, 2007), 72.

13 Barad, 73.

14 Jennifer Gabrys, Gay Hawkins, and Mike Michael, eds., introduction to *Accumulation: The Material Politics of Plastic* (London: Routledge, 2013), 3.

15 Eduardo Kohn, *How Forests Think: Toward an Anthropology beyond the Human* (Berkeley: University of California Press, 2013), 59.

16 Kohn, 41, 42, 62.

17 Kohn, 74, 75.

18 Kohn, 76, 81.

19 James C. Scott, *Seeing Like a State* (New Haven, Conn.: Yale University Press, 1998), 13, 15.

20 Scott, 19.

21 Peter Larkin, *Terrain Seed Scarcity: Poems from a Decade* (Cambridge: Salt, 2001), 55.

22 Timothy Luke, "On Environmentality: Geo-power and Eco-knowledge in the Discourses of Contemporary Environmentalism," *Cultural Critique* 31 (1995): 64.

23 Tsing, *Mushroom at the End of the World,* 134.

24 Moore, *Capitalism in the Web of Life,* 11, 12.

25 Tsing, *Mushroom at the End of the World,* 40.

26 Peter Larkin, *Lessways Least Scarce Among: Poems 2002–2002* (Exeter, U.K.: Shearsman Books, 2012), 8.

27 Harriet Tarlo, ed., introduction to *The Ground Aslant: An Anthology of Radical Landscape Poetry* (Exeter, U.K.: Shearsman Books, 2011), 7.

28 Larkin, *Lessways Least Scarce Among,* 8.

29 See Mandy Bloomfield, "Landscaping the Page: British Open-Field Poetics and Environmental Aesthetics," *Green Letters* 17, no. 2 (2013): 121–36.

30 Karen Barad, "Diffracting Difference: Cutting Together-Apart," *Parallax* 20, no. 3 (2014): 168.

31 Larkin, *Lessways Least Scarce Among,* 14.

32 Peter Larkin, in Edmund Hardy, "Less Than, More At: An Interview with Peter Larkin," *Intercapillary Space* (blog), 2010, http://intercapil-laryspace.blogspot.co.uk/.

33 Barad, *Meeting the Universe,* 30, 93.

34 Jonathan Skinner, "Poetries of the Third Landscape," in *) ((eco(lang) (uage (reader)),* ed. Brenda Iijima (Callicoon, N.Y.: Portable Press at yo-yo labs/Nightboat Books, 2010), 37.

35 Larkin, "Fully From, All Scarce To," *ecopoetics* 4/5 (2004): 113.

36 Larkin, 115.

37 Larkin, *Terrain Seed Scarcity,* 107.

38 Hardy, "Less Than, More At."

39 Moore, *Capitalism in the Web of Life,* 44.

40 Peter Larkin, "Scarcity by Gift: Horizons of the 'Lucy' Poems," *The Coleridge Bulletin* 23 (2004): 50.

41 Timothy Mitchell, *Carbon Democracy: Political Power in the Age of Oil* (London: Verso, 2011).

42 Peter Larkin in "Matthew Hall Interviews Peter Larkin," *Cordite Poetry Review,* August 1, 2010, http://cordite.org.au/.

43 Larkin, "Scarcity by Gift," 51.

44 Hardy, "Less Than, More At."

45 John Kinsella, *Disclosed Poetics* (Manchester, U.K.: Manchester University Press, 2007), 12.

46 Robert Frost, *The Poetry of Robert Frost* (London: Jonathan Cape, 1971), 33.

47 Larkin, *Lessways Least Scarce Among,* 39.

48 Larkin, 14.

49 Larkin, 22.

50 Larkin, *Terrain Seed Scarcity,* 115.

51 Larkin, 121.

52 Larkin, 120, 118.

53 Larkin, *Lessways Least Scarce Among,* 14.

54 Larkin, *Terrain Seed Scarcity,* 108.

55 Larkin, "Less Than, More At."

56 Terry Gifford, *Pastoral* (London: Routledge, 1999), 148.

57 Larkin, *Terrain Seed Scarcity,* 107.

58 Larkin, *Lessways Least Scarce Among,* 14.

59 Larkin, 14.

60 Larkin, *Terrain Seed Scarcity*, 123.

61 Larkin, 124.

62 Tsing, *Mushroom at the End of the World*, 24.

63 Larkin, *Terrain Seed Scarcity*, 113, 123.

64 Robert P. Baird, "Review: Leaves of Field," *Chicago Review* 53, no. 1 (2007): 186.

65 Larkin, *Terrain Seed Scarcity*, 123.

66 Larkin, 130.

67 Tsing, "On Nonscalability," 508.

68 Tsing, *Mushroom at the End of the World*, 20.

69 Barad, "Diffracting Difference," 169, 168.

70 Larkin, *Lessways Least Scarce Among*, 19–20.

71 Anna Tsing, "Blasted Landscapes (and the Gentle Art of Mushroom Picking)," in *The Multispecies Salon*, ed. Eben Kirksey (Durham, N.C.: Duke University Press, 2014), 92.

72 Tsing, 92.

73 Tsing, *Mushroom at the End of the World*, 152.

74 Tsing, 142.

75 Peter Larkin, *Leaves of Field* (Exeter, U.K.: Shearsman: 2004), 45.

76 Peter Larkin, *Give Forest Its Next Portent* (Exeter, U.K.: Shearsman, 2014), 9.

77 Larkin, 124.

78 Larkin, 126.

79 Larkin, 112.

80 Tsing, *Mushroom at the End of the World*, 152.

81 Tsing, 168.

82 Tsing, 170.

83 Larkin, *Lessways Least Scarce Among*, 39.

84 Larkin, 11.

85 Larkin, 12.

86 Barad, *Meeting the Universe Halfway*, 72.

87 Klein, *This Changes Everything*, 172, 222.

88 Etienne Benson, "Generating Infrastructural Invisibility: Insulation, Interconnection, and Avian Excrement in the Southern Californian Power Grid," *Environmental Humanities* 6 (2015): 125.

89 Benson, 111–16.

90 Larkin, *Lessways Least Scarce Among*, 11, 12.

91 Benson, "Generating Infrastructural Invisibility," 109.

92 Jane Bennett, "The Agency of Assemblages and the North American Blackout," *Public Culture* 17, no. 3 (2005): 446.

93 Barad, *Meeting the Universe Halfway,* 30.

94 Peter Larkin, "Plantations Parallels Apart," in *Terrain Seed Scarcity,* 107.

95 Larkin, *Leaves of Field,* 9.

96 Sjef van Gaalen, "Fungal Products Won't Win Prizes for Glamour but Will Be Greener," *New Scientist,* April 27, 2016, https://www.new scientist.com/; see also http://www.corpuscoli.com/.

97 Chiara Alessi, "The Future of Plastic," *DOMUS,* June 24, 2016, http://www.domusweb.it/.

98 van Gaalen, "Fungal Products."

99 Roland Barthes, *Mythologies,* trans. Annette Lavers (1973; repr., London: Paladin, 1987), 97.

100 Jeffrey L. Meikle, "Material Doubts: The Consequences of Plastic," *Environmental History* 2, no. 3 (1997): 278.

101 Bernadette Bensaude-Vincent, "Plastics, Materials and Dreams of Dematerialisation," in Gabrys et al., *Accumulation,* 23.

102 Bensaude-Vincent et al., 18.

103 Jody A. Roberts, "Reflections of an Unrepentant Plastiphobe: Plasticity and STS Life," *Science as Culture* 19, no. 1 (2010): 106.

104 Adam Dickinson, "Energy Humanities and Metabolic Poetics," *Review in Cultural Theory* 6, no. 3 (2016): 20.

105 Andrew Barry, "Pharmaceutical Matters: The Invention of Informed Materials," *Theory, Culture, and Society* 22, no. 1 (2005): 56.

106 Bernadette Bensaude-Vincent and Isabelle Stengers, *A History of Chemistry* (Cambridge, Mass.: Harvard University Press, 1996), 206.

107 James Marriott and Mika Minio-Paluello, "Where Does This Stuff Come From? Oil, Plastic, and the Distribution of Violence," in Gabrys et al., *Accumulation,* 180.

108 Anthony Andrady, *Plastics and Environmental Sustainability* (Hoboken, N.J.: John Wiley, 2015), 146.

109 See Roberts, "Reflections of an Unrepentant Plastiphobe."

110 Gabrys et al., introduction to *Accumulation,* 6.

111 Serenella Iovino and Serpil Oppermann, "Stories Come to Matter," in *Material Ecocriticism,* ed. Serenella Iovino and Serpil Oppermann (Bloomington: Indiana University Press, 2014), 1.

112 Evelyn Reilly, in Angela Hume, "Imaging Ecopoetics: An Interview with Robert Hass, Brenda Hillman, Evelyn Reilly, and Jonathan Skinner," *ISLE* 19, no. 4 (2013): 764.

113 Heather Davis, "Life and Death in the Anthropocene: A Short History of Plastic," in *Art in the Anthropocene,* ed. Heather Davis and Etienne Turpin (London: Open Humanities Press, 2015), 349.

114 Barthes, *Mythologies,* 97.
115 Moore, *Capitalism in the Web of Life,* 44; Jeffrey Meikle, *American Plastic: A Cultural History* (New Brunswick, N.J.: Rutgers University Press, 1995), 45.
116 Gabrys et al., introduction, 5.
117 Evelyn Reilly, *Styrofoam* (New York: Roof Books, 2009), 30.
118 Reilly, 20.
119 Lynn Keller, "The Ecopoetics of Hyperobjects," *ISLE* 22, no. 4 (2015): 850.
120 J. Hillis Miller, "The Poetics of Cyberspace," in *Contemporary Poetics,* ed. Louis Armand (Evanston, Ill.: Northwestern University Press, 2007), 256.
121 McKenzie Wark, "From Hypertext to Codework," in Armand, *Contemporary Poetics,* 283.
122 Wark, 56.
123 Wark, 58.
124 Reilly, *Styrofoam,* 48.
125 Reilly, 12
126 Reilly, 17.
127 Reilly, 11.
128 Reilly, 61.
129 Herman Melville, *Moby-Dick, or The Whale* (London: Penguin, 1992), 205.
130 Melville, 61.
131 Evelyn Reilly, "Environmental Dreamscapes and Ecopoetic Grief," *Omniverse,* Spring 2013, http://omniverse.us/.
132 Reilly, *Styrofoam,* 9.
133 Davis, "Life and Death in the Anthropocene," 352.
134 Tom Fisher, "The Death and Life of Plastic Surfaces," in Gabrys et al., *Accumulation,* 108.
135 Reilly, *Styrofoam,* 64, emphasis original. See Melville, *Moby-Dick,* 210.
136 Gabrys et al., introduction, 5.
137 Jamie, "Interview."
138 Christian Sonne et al., "Xenoendocrine Pollutants May Reduce Size of Sexual Organs in East Greenland Polar Bears *(Ursus maritimus),*" *Environmental Science and Technology* 40, no. 18 (2006): 5668–74.
139 Reilly, *Styrofoam,* 68.
140 D. H. Lawrence, *Last Poems,* ed. Richard Aldington (London: Martin Secker, 1933), 60–64.
141 Andrady, *Plastics and Environmental Sustainability,* 297.

142 Shige Takada, "International Pellet Watch," in Gabrys et al., *Accumulation*, 192.

143 Marcus Erikson et al., "Plastic Pollution in the World's Oceans: More than 5 Trillion Plastic Pieces Weighing over 250,000 Tons Afloat at Sea," *PLoS ONE* 9, no. 12 (2014): 1–15, http://journals.plos.org/; Lucy C. Woodall, Anna Sanchez-Vidal, Miquel Canals, Gordon L. J. Paterson, Rachel Coppock, Victoria Sleight, Antonio Calafat, Alex D. Rogers, Bhavani E. Narayanaswamy, and Richard C. Thompson, "The Deep Sea Is a Major Sink for Microplastic Debris," *Royal Society Open Science* 1 (2014): 140317, http://rsos.royalsocietypublishing.org/.

144 Jennifer Gabrys, "Plastic Waste and the Work of the Biodegradable," in Gabrys et al., *Accumulation*, 216.

145 Erik R. Zettler, Tracy J. Mincer, and Linda A. Amaral-Zettler, "Life in the 'Plastisphere': Microbial Communities on Plastic Marine Debris," *Environmental Science and Technology* 47 (2013): 7137–46.

146 Fisher, "Death and Life of Plastic Surfaces," 111.

147 Slavoj Žižek, *The Parallax View* (Cambridge, Mass.: MIT Press, 2006), 62, emphasis original.

148 Gay Hawkins, "Made to Be Wasted: PET and Topologies of Disposability," in Gabrys et al., *Accumulation*, 50.

149 Myra J. Hird, "Waste, Landfills, and an Environmental Ethics of Vulnerability," *Ethics and the Environment* 18, no. 1 (2003): 107, 113.

150 Reilly, *Styrofoam*, 11.

151 Melville, *Moby-Dick*, 206.

152 Reilly, *Styrofoam*, 10.

153 See http://www.chrisjordan.com/.

154 Stacy Alaimo, *Bodily Natures: Science, Environment, and the Material Self* (Bloomington: Indiana University Press, 2010), 487, 488.

155 Thom van Dooren, *Flight Ways: Life and Loss at the Edge of Extinction* (London: Columbia University Press, 2014), 24.

156 van Dooren, 31.

157 van Dooren, 33, 32.

158 Adam Dickinson, *The Polymers* (Toronto: House of Anansi Press, 2013), 7.

159 Reilly, *Styrofoam*, 12.

160 Jayna Brown, "Being Cellular: Race, the Inhuman, and the Plasticity of Life," *GLQ* 21, no. 2–3 (2015): 321.

161 Brown, 323.

162 Hannah Landecker, *Culturing Life* (Cambridge, Mass.: Harvard University Press, 2007), 18.

163 Brown, "Being Cellular," 322.
164 Paul Gilroy, *Between Camps: Nations, Cultures, and the Allure of Race* (London: Allen Lane, 2000), 19.
165 Reilly, *Styrofoam,* 44–45.
166 Jahan Ramazani, *Poetry of Mourning: The Modern Elegy from Hardy to Heaney* (Chicago: University of Chicago Press, 1994), 3.
167 Reilly, *Styrofoam,* 42.
168 Reilly, 45.
169 Reilly, 43.
170 Rebecca Altman, "American Petro-topia," *Aeon,* https:/aeon.co/.
171 Tsing, *Mushroom at the End of the World,* 5.
172 Tsing, 142.
173 Zettler et al., "Life in the 'Plastisphere,'" 7137–46.

3. SWERVE

1 Stephen Greenblatt, *The Swerve: How the World Became Modern* (New York: W. W. Norton, 2011), 7.
2 Donna Haraway, *When Species Meet* (Minneapolis: University of Minnesota Press, 2008), 5.
3 Lynn Margulis, *Symbiotic Planet* (Amherst, N.Y.: Basic Books, 1998), 20.
4 Margulis, 37.
5 Deborah Bird Rose, *Wild Dog Dreaming: Love and Extinction* (Charlottesville: University of Virginia Press, 2011), 122.
6 Jean-Luc Nancy, *The Inoperative Community,* trans. Peter Connor, Lisa Garbus, Michael Holland, and Simona Sawhney (Minneapolis: University of Minnesota Press, 1991), 4, 3.
7 Alfred Jarry, *The Selected Works of Alfred Jarry,* ed. Roger Shattuck and Simon Watson Taylor (London: Methuen, 1965), 238.
8 Deborah Bird Rose, "Multispecies Knots of Ethical Time," *Environmental Philosophy* 9, no. 1 (2012): 130–31.
9 Thom van Dooren, Eben Kirksey, and Ursula Münster, "Multispecies Studies: Cultivating Arts of Attentiveness," *Environmental Humanities* 8, no. 1 (2016): 2.
10 Rose, "Multispecies Knots of Ethical Time," 128.
11 Deborah Bird Rose, "What If the Angel of History Were a Dog?," *Cultural Studies Review* 12, no. 1 (2006): 75.
12 Henrique M. Pereira et al., "Scenarios for Global Biodiversity in the 21st Century," *Science* 330, no. 6010 (2010): 1496–501, http://science.sciencemag.org/.

13 Edward O. Wilson, "Biophilia and the Conservation Ethic," in *The Biophilia Hypothesis,* ed. Stephen R. Kellert and Edward O. Wilson (Washington, D.C.: Island Press/Shearwater Books, 1993), 37.

14 Caitlin Berrigan, "Life Cycle of a Common Weed," in *The Multispecies Salon,* ed. Eben Kirksey (Durham, N.C.: Duke University Press, 2014), 169.

15 Thom van Dooren, "A Day with Crows—Rarity, Nativity, and the Violent-Care of Conservation," *Animal Studies* 4, no. 2 (2015): 16.

16 Donna Haraway, *Staying with the Trouble* (Durham, N.C.: Duke University Press, 2016), 32.

17 Rose, *Wild Dog Dreaming,* 11.

18 Walter Benjamin, "On Language as Such and on the Language of Man," in *Reflections,* trans. Edmund Jephcott (New York: Schocken Books, 1986), 316.

19 Kelsey Green and Franklin Ginn, "The Smell of Selfless Love: Sharing Vulnerability with Bees in Alternative Apiculture," *Environmental Humanities* 4 (2014): 168.

20 Gaia Vince, "Jellyfish Blooms Creating Oceans of Slime," BBC, April 5, 2012, http://www.bbc.com/.

21 Les Murray, *Collected Poems* (Manchester, U.K.: Carcanet, 2003), 528.

22 Mark Schrope, "Attack of the Blobs," *Nature* 482 (2012): 20; Lucas Brotz, William W. L. Cheung, Kristin Kleisner, Evgeny Pakhomov, and Daniel Pauly, "Increasing Jellyfish Populations: Trends in Large Marine Eocsystems," *Hydrobiologia* 690 (2012): 3–20.

23 Anthony J. Richardson, Andrew Bakun, Graeme C. Hays, and Mark J. Gibbons, "The Jellyfish Joyride: Causes, Consequences and Management Responses to a More Gelatinous Future," *Trends in Ecology and Evolution* 24, no. 6 (2006): 318.

24 Joseph Masco, *The Nuclear Borderlands: The Manhattan Project in Post–Cold War New Mexico* (Princeton, N.J.: Princeton University Press, 2006), 28.

25 Richardson et al., "Jellyfish Joyride," 317–18.

26 Brotz et al., "Increasing Jellyfish Populations," 3.

27 See Schrope, "Attack of the Blobs"; Richardson et al., "Jellyfish Joyride"; Jennifer Purcell, "Jellyfish and Ctenophore Blooms Coincide with Human Proliferations and Environmental Perturbations," *Annual Review of Marine Science* 4 (2012): 209–35.

28 Purcell, 223.

29 Elizabeth Johnson, "Governing Jellyfish: Eco-security and Planetary 'Life' in the Anthropocene," in *Animals, Biopolitics, Law: Lively Legalities,* ed. Irus Braverman (London: Routledge, 2015), 64. Not all observers are

convinced that there is an increase in jellyfish blooms. Jellyfish natural history is patchy at best. Their soft bodies make them difficult to catch and also mean that they do not often leave fossils. Robert Condon suggests that anecdotal evidence of an increase in blooms is simply part of a longer cycle, a slow pulse that has coincided with a rise in human interest. Jennifer Purcell distinguishes between an increase in populations and the fact that "human problems with jellyfish have increased recently." Nonetheless, as Gaia Vince observes, "what is clear is that jellyfish are simply better prepared than other marine life for many of the ways humans are changing the ocean environment." Robert H. Condon, Carlos M. Duarte, Kylie A. Pitt, Kelly L. Robinson, Cathy H. Lucas, Kelly R. Sutherland, Hermes W. Mianzan et al., "Recurrent Jellyfish Blooms Are a Consequence of Global Oscillations," *PNAS* 110, no. 3 (2013): 1000–1005; Purcell, "Jellyfish and Ctenophore Blooms," 210; Vince, "Jellyfish Blooms Creating Oceans of Slime."

30 Jean Sprackland, *Hard Water* (London: Random House, 2011), 48.
31 Stacy Alaimo, "Jellyfish Science, Jellyfish Aesthetics: Posthuman Reconfigurations of the Sensible," in *Thinking with Water*, ed. Cecilia Chen, Janine McLeod, and Astrida Neimanis (Montreal: McGill-Queen's University Press, 2013), 139, 153.
32 Eva Hayward, "Sensational Jellyfish: Aquarium Affects and the Matter of Immersion," *differences* 23, no. 5 (2012): 177.
33 Alaimo, "Jellyfish Science, Jellyfish Aesthetics," 152.
34 Mark Doty, *My Alexandria* (London: Cape Poetry, 1995), 44.
35 Kate Rigby, "Earth, World, Text: On the (Im)possibility of Ecopoiesis," *New Literary History* 35, no. 3 (2004): 437.
36 Paul Ricoeur, "The Metaphorical Process as Cognition, Imagination, and Feeling," *Critical Inquiry* 5, no. 1 (1978): 145.
37 Doty, *My Alexandria*, 45.
38 Ricoeur, "Metaphorical Process," 148.
39 Erich Auerbach, *Scenes from the Drama of European Literature* (1959; repr., Minneapolis: University of Minnesota Press, 1984), 11, 12.
40 Haraway, *When Species Meet*, 4.
41 Jonathan Culler, *The Pursuit of Signs* (London: Routledge, 2001), 233.
42 Jonathan Culler, *Theory of the Lyric* (Cambridge, Mass.: Harvard University Press, 2015), 242.
43 Johnson, "Governing Jellyfish," 70.
44 Donna Haraway, "The Promises of Monsters: A Regenerative Politics for Inappropriate/d Others," in *Cultural Studies*, ed. L. Grossberg, C. Nelson, and P. A. Treichler (New York: Routledge, 1992), 300.
45 Hayward, "Sensational Jellyfish," 182.

46 Hayward, 162, 182.

47 Doty, *My Alexandria,* 45.

48 Alison Benjamin, Amanda Holpuch, and Ruth Spencer, "Buzzfeeds: The Effects of Colony Collapse Disorder and Other Bee News," *Guardian,* July 30, 2013, https://www.theguardian.com/.

49 Alison Benjamin and Brian McCallum, *A World without Bees* (London: Guardian Books, 2009), 7.

50 United Nations Environment Programme, "Global Honey Bee Colony Disorders and Other Threats to Insect Pollinators," http://www.unep.org/.

51 NRDC, "Why We Need Bees: Nature's Tiny Workers Put Food on Our Tables," https://www.nrdc.org/.

52 Walsh, "Trouble with Beekeeping in the Anthropocene," *Time,* August 9, 2013, http://www.science.time.com/.

53 Lisa Jean Moore and Mary Kosut, "Among the Colony: Ethnographic Fieldwork, Urban Bees, and Intra-species Mindfulness," *Ethnography* 15, no. 4 (2014): 517.

54 Freya Matthews, "Planet Beehive," *Australian Humanities Review* 50 (2011), http://www.australianhumanitiesreview.org/.

55 Eric C. Brown, "Reading the Insect," in *Insect Poetics,* ed. Eric C. Brown (Minneapolis: University of Minnesota Press, 2006), ix, x.

56 Virgil, *The Georgics of Virgil,* trans. C. Day Lewis (London: Jonathan Cape, 1940), 77.

57 William Shakespeare, *Henry V,* act 1, scene 2, ll. 188–89.

58 Matthews, "Planet Beehive." See also E. O. Wilson and Bert Hölldobler, *The Superorganism* (New York: W. W. Norton, 2008).

59 Hugh Raffles, *Insectopedia* (New York: Vintage, 2010), 173.

60 Jake Kosek, "Ecologies of Empire: On the Uses of the Honeybee," *Cultural Anthropology* 25, no. 4 (2010): 651.

61 Masco has reported how the U.S. Department of Energy's Long Term Stewardship Program has deployed honeybees as "an environmental tool" since the 1970s, to track the presence of radionuclides in parts of New Mexico irradiated during nuclear weapons tests. Joseph Masco, "Mutant Ecologies: Radioactive Life in Post–Cold War New Mexico," *Cultural Anthropology* 19, no. 4 (2004): 537.

62 Kosek, "Ecologies of Empire," 663, emphasis added.

63 Alyssa N. Crittenden, "The Importance of Honey Consumption in Human Evolution," *Food and Foodways* 19, no. 4 (2011): 257–73.

64 Paul Muldoon, *The End of the Poem: Oxford Lectures* (New York: Farrar, Strauss, and Giroux, 2006), 59.

65 Sean Borodale, email to the author, October 27, 2015.

66 Sean Borodale, introduction to *Bee Journal* (London: Vintage, 2016), xvii.

67 Sean Borodale, Scottish Poetry Library podcast, November 2012, 45:25, http://www.spl.org.uk/.

68 Sean Borodale, *Bee Journal* (London: Cape Poetry, 2012), 62.

69 Culler, *Theory of the Lyric,* 294.

70 Borodale, email, October 27, 2015.

71 Borodale, *Bee Journal,* 1.

72 Borodale, SPL podcast.

73 Borodale, *Bee Journal,* 64. Brown notes that insect otherness is in part due to their speed of reproduction, such that they might seem to "evolve before our eyes, as if they are outstripping the advances of our prolonged lives." Yet this "uncanny temporality" has been overtaken by the evolutionary effects of bees' shared recent history with us. Brown, "Reading the Insect," xii.

74 Borodale, SPL podcast.

75 Borodale, *Bee Journal,* 4.

76 Borodale, 6, 28, 87, 49, emphasis original.

77 Borodale, 6, 8.

78 Borodale, email, October 27, 2015.

79 Borodale, *Bee Journal,* 4–5.

80 Richard Cureton, "Rhythm, Temporality, and 'Inner Form,'" *Style* 49, no. 1 (2015): 85.

81 Borodale, SPL podcast.

82 Borodale.

83 Henri Meschonnic, quoted in Marjorie Perloff, *Poetry On and Off the Page* (Evanston, Ill.: Northwestern University Press, 1998), 136.

84 Perloff, 139.

85 Borodale, email, October 27, 2015.

86 T. V. F. Brogan, "Trochaic," in *The Princeton Encyclopaedia of Poetry and Poetics,* 4th ed., ed. Roland Green et al. (Princeton, N.J.: Princeton University Press, 2012), 1462.

87 Bees that have discovered a rich food source will communicate the location and value of the source via a dance that conveys information about its direction and distance from the hive. Direction is indicated in relation to the position of the sun; a dancing bee must therefore adjust the dance depending on how far the sun has traveled in the time the bee took to return to the hive. According to Eileen Crist, the dance language has both symbolic and performative force, a form of telling that indicates that bees possess a spatial and temporal imaginary. Crist, "Can an Insect Speak? The Case of the Honey Bee Dance Language," *Social Studies of Science*

34, no. 7 (2004): 25, 26; see also Karl von Frisch, *The Dance Language and Orientation of Bees* (Cambridge, Mass.: Harvard University Press, 1967); Martin Lindauer, *Communication among Social Bees* (Cambridge, Mass.: Harvard University Press, 1961); James L. Gould and Carol Grant Gould, *The Honey Bee* (New York: Scientific American Library, 1988).

88 Crist, "Can an Insect Speak?," 26.

89 Karl von Frisch, *The Dancing Bees,* trans. Dora Isle (London: Methuen, 1954), 147.

90 Muldoon, *End of the Poem,* 9.

91 Borodale, *Bee Journal,* 16.

92 Borodale, email, October 27, 2015.

93 Culler, *Theory of the Lyric,* 161.

94 Culler, 212.

95 Borodale, *Bee Journal,* 4.

96 Mutlu Konuk Blasing, *Lyric Poetry* (Princeton, N.J.: Princeton University Press, 2007), 30, 53.

97 Haraway, *When Species Meet,* 4.

98 Borodale, *Bee Journal,* 2.

99 Culler, *Theory of the Lyric,* 225.

100 Borodale, *Bee Journal,* 4.

101 Borodale, 4, emphasis added.

102 Borodale, SPL podcast.

103 Borodale, *Bee Journal,* 63.

104 Borodale, 8.

105 Borodale, 49.

106 Borodale, 43.

107 Borodale, 55, emphasis original.

108 Borodale, 67.

109 Borodale, 48.

110 Harold Bloom, "*Clinamen,* or Poetic Misprision," *New Literary History* 3, no. 2 (1972): 381.

111 Mary Lefkowitz, "On Bees, Poets, and Plato: Ancient Biographers' Representations of the Creative Process," in *Creative Lives in Classical Antiquity,* ed. Richard Fletcher and Johanna Hanink (Cambridge: Cambridge University Press, 2016), 182; Elizabeth Atwood Lawrence, "The Scared Bee, the Filth Pig, and the Bat out of Hell: Animal Symbolism in Cognitive Biophilia," in *The Biophilia Hypothesis,* ed. Stephen R. Kellert and Edward O. Wilson (Washington, D.C.: Island Press/Shearwater Books, 1993), 302.

112 Bruno Latour, *Pandora's Hope: Essays on the Reality of Science Studies* (Cambridge, Mass.: Harvard University Press, 1999), 280.

113 Latour, 189.
114 Borodale, *Bee Journal,* 27.
115 Borodale, 78.
116 Catriona Sandilands, "Pro/Polis: Three Forays into the Political Lives of Bees," in *Material Ecocriticism,* ed. Serenella Iovino and Serpil Oppermann (Bloomington: Indiana University Press, 2014), 167.
117 Richard Nimmo, "Apiculture in the Anthropocene: Between Posthumanism and Critical Animal Studies," in *Animals in the Anthropocene,* ed. Human Animal Research Network Editorial Collective (Sydney: Sydney University Press, 2015), 187–88, 184.
118 Matthews, "Planet Beehive."
119 Borodale, SPL podcast.
120 Borodale, *Bee Journal,* 56.
121 Matthews, "Planet Beehive."
122 Borodale, email, October 27, 2015.
123 Pak Chung Wong, Kwong-Kwok Wong, and Harlan Foote, "Organic Data Memory: Using the DNA Approach," *Communications of the ACM* 46, no. 1 (2003): 95–98.
124 Natasha McDowell, "Data Stored in Multiplying Bacteria," *New Scientist,* January 8, 2003, https://www.newscientist.com/.
125 Wong et al., "Organic Data Memory," 98.
126 Sylvestre Marillonnet, Victor Klimyuk, and Yuri Gleba, "Encoding Technical Information in GM Organisms," *Nature Biotechnology* 21 (2003): 224–26.
127 Jeannie Vanasco, "Literary Immortality through DNA Coding: An Investigation," *The New Yorker,* March 24, 2011, http://www.newyorker.com/.
128 Andy Extance, "How DNA Could Store All the World's Data," *Nature* 357 (2016): 22–24.
129 Patrick House, "Object of Interest: The Twice-Forbidden Fruit," *The New Yorker,* May 13, 2014, http://www.newyorker.com/.
130 Ed Yong, "This Speck of DNA Contains a Movie, a Computer Virus, and an Amazon Gift Card," *The Atlantic,* March 2, 2017, https://www.theatlantic.com/.
131 Jay Clayton, "Genome Time," in *Time and the Literary,* ed. Karen Newman, Jay Clayton, and Marianne Hirsch (London: Routledge, 2013), 33.
132 Jay Clayton, "Genome Time: Post-Darwinism Then and Now," *Critical Quarterly* 55, no. 1 (2013): 58.
133 Donna Haraway, *Modest_Witness@Second_Millenium.FemaleMan©_Meets_OncoMouse™* (London: Routledge, 1997), 142, 134.

134 Evelyn Fox Keller, "Genes, Genomes, and Genomics," *Biological Theory* 6, no. 2 (2011): 139. Elsewhere, Keller denies that genes possess agency apart from the networks they interact with. "By themselves, the entities we call genes do not act; they do not have agency. Strictly speaking, the very notion of a gene as an autonomous element, as an entity that exists in its own right, is a fiction. In order for a sequence of nucleotides to become what is conventionally called a gene requires that the sequence be embedded in a cellular complex that not only reads, translates, and interprets that sequence, but also defines it, giving it its very meaning." Evelyn Fox Keller, *The Mirage of the Space between Nature and Nurture* (Durham, N.C.: Duke University Press, 2010), 6.

135 Haraway, *Modest_Witness*, 142.

136 Stefan Helmreich, *Alien Ocean: Anthropological Voyages in Microbial Seas* (Berkeley: University of California Press, 2009), 60.

137 Haraway, *Modest_Witness*, 137.

138 Greenblatt, *Swerve*, 7.

139 Christian Bök, "The Untimeliness of the Xenotext," *Harriet Blog*, April 11, 2010, https://www.poetryfoundation.org/.

140 Christian Bök, "From *The Xenotext*," in *The Routledge Companion to the Environmental Humanities*, ed. Ursula K. Heise, Jon Christensen, and Michelle Niemann (London: Routledge, 2017), 393. This is an extract from the as-yet-unpublished *The Xenotext: Book 2*.

141 Roya Saffary et al., "Microbial Survival of Space Vacuum and Extreme Ultraviolet Irradiation: Strain Isolation and Analysis during a Rocket Flight," *FEMS Microbiology Letters* 215 (2002): 163–68.

142 Bök, "From *The Xenotext*," 394.

143 Christian Bök, *The Xenotext: Book 1* (Toronto: Coach House Books, 2015), 151.

144 Bök, 150.

145 To date, Bök has succeeded in encoding the poems in a strain of *E. coli* but not yet in *D. radiodurans*.

146 Elizabeth Sewell, in Robert McGahey, *The Orphic Moment: Shaman to Poet-Thinker in Plato, Nietzsche, and Mallarmé* (Albany: State University of New York, 1994), 3.

147 Rainer Maria Rilke, *Sonnets to Orpheus* (London: Hogarth Press, 1957), 85.

148 Rilke, 89, 115.

149 Julian Murphet, "Poetry in the Medium of Life: Text, Code, Organism," in *Writing, Medium, Machine: Modern Technologies*, ed. Sean Pryor and David Trotter (Open Humanities Press, 2016), 211; William Shakespeare, *Sonnets* (Cambridge: Cambridge University Press, 1967), 12.

150 Shakespeare, 3, 43.

151 Nikki Skillman, *The Lyric in the Age of the Brain* (Cambridge, Mass.: Harvard University Press, 2016), 261.

152 Ada Smailbegović, "Poetics of Liveliness: Natural Histories of Matter and Change in Twentieth and Twenty-First Century Poetry" (PhD diss., New York University, 2015), 85, 90.

153 John Charles Ryan, "Biological Processes as Writerly? An Ecological Critique of DNA-Based Poetry," *Environmental Humanities* 9, no. 1 (2017): 129–48.

154 Robert Majzels, "The Xenotext Experiment and the Gift of Death," *Jacket 2*, March 29, 2013, http://jacket2.org/.

155 Skillman, *Lyric in the Age of the Brain*, 264; Smailbegović, "Poetics of Liveliness," 87.

156 According to Roof, "DNA's metaphors . . . conserve a particular way of seeing and understanding the world in the face of more complex and unfamiliar possibilities." Judith Roof, *The Poetics of DNA* (Minneapolis: University of Minnesota Press, 2007), 65.

157 Bök, *Xenotext: Book 1*, 153.

158 Bök, 141.

159 Roof, *Poetics of DNA*, 26.

160 Bök, *Xenotext: Book 1*, 156, 144, 141.

161 Peter Middleton, "Epigenetics and Poetry: Challenges to Genetic Determinism in Michael Byers's *Long for This World* and Mei-mei Berssenbrugge's 'The Four Year Old Girl,'" *Textual Practice* 29, no. 3 (2015): 517–45.

162 Bök, "From *The Xenotext*," 400, emphasis added.

163 Alfred Jarry, *The Selected Works of Alfred Jarry*, ed. Roger Shattuck and Simon Watson Taylor (London: Methuen, 1965), 193.

164 Christian Bök, "'Pataphysics: The Poetics of an Imaginary Science" (PhD thesis, York University, 1997), 3.

165 Bök, "Untimeliness of the Xenotext."

166 Bök, conversation with the author.

167 Marjorie Perloff, *Radical Artifice: Writing Poetry in the Age of Media* (Chicago: University of Chicago Press, 1991), 140.

168 Christian Bök, in Krista Zala, "Q&A: Poetry in the Genes," *Nature* 458, no. 5 (2009): 35.

169 Darren Wershler, "The Xenotext Experiment, So Far," *Canadian Journal of Communication* 37, no. 1 (2012): 50.

170 Myra J. Hird, *The Origins of Sociable Life: Evolution after Science Studies* (Basingstoke, U.K.: Palgrave Macmillan, 2009), 42, 46.

171 Benjamin, "On Language as Such," 316.

172 Bök, conversation with the author.
173 Christian Bök, in Alexander Kim, "The Xenotext Experiment," Triple Helix Online: A Global Forum for Science and Society, January 8, 2014, http://triplehelixblog.com/.
174 Bök, "Untimeliness of the Xenotext."
175 Bök, "'Pataphysics," 10.
176 Marjorie Perloff, *Unoriginal Genius: Poetry by Other Means* (Chicago: University of Chicago Press, 2010), 11.
177 Bök, *Xenotext: Book 1,* 46, 74.
178 Emily Dickinson, *The Works of Emily Dickinson* (Hertfordshire, U.K.: Wordsworth, 1994), 149.
179 Susan Stewart, *Poetry and the Fate of the Sense* (Chicago: University of Chicago Press, 2002), 257.
180 John Keats, *The Complete Poetry and Selected Prose of John Keats* (New York: Modern Library, 1951), 172.
181 Bök, *Xenotext: Book 1,* 100–102.
182 Timothy Morton, "The Dark Ecology of Elegy," in *The Oxford Handbook of the Elegy,* ed. Karen Weisman (Oxford: Oxford University Press, 2010), 251, 254.
183 Bonnie Costello, "Fresh Woods: Elegy and Ecology among the Ruins," in Weisman, *Oxford Handbook of the Elegy,* 330.
184 Christian Bök, "Orpheus" and "Eurydice" (unpublished poems).
185 Skillman, *Lyric in the Age of the Brain,* 265.
186 Wershler, "Xenotext Experiment, So Far," 51; Skillman, *Lyric in the Age of the Brain,* 266.
187 Leon Jaroff, "The Gene Hunt," *Time,* March 20, 1989, 67.
188 Murphet, "Poetry in the Medium of Life," 221.
189 W. B. Yeats, *The Poems* (London: Everyman, 1990), 87, 59.
190 Skillman, *Lyric in the Age of the Brain,* 266.
191 W. B. Yeats, "The Celtic Element in Literature," in *Early Essays,* vol. 4 of *The Collected Works of WB Yeats,* ed. George Bornstein and Richard J. Finnerman (New York: Scribner, 2007), 132.
192 W. B. Yeats, "William Blake and the Imagination," in *Early Essays,* 85.
193 William Blake, in *The Romantic Period,* vol. D of *The Norton Anthology of English Literature,* ed. Deidre Shauna Lynch and Jack Stillinger (New York: W. W. Norton, 2012), 128.
194 Maurice Blanchot, *The Gaze of Orpheus and Other Literary Essays,* trans. Lydia Davis (New York: Station Hill Press, 1981), 99.
195 HD, *Collected Poems 1912–1944* (New York: New Directions Books, 1983), 52.

196 HD, 55.

197 R. Clifton Spargo, *The Ethics of Mourning: Grief and Responsibility in Elegiac Literature* (Baltimore: The Johns Hopkins University Press, 2004), 4; Costello, "Fresh Woods," 330.

198 Morton, "Dark Ecology of Elegy," 254.

199 Avery Gordon, "Some Thoughts on Haunting and Futurity," *borderlands* 10, no. 2 (2011): 4, http://borderlands.net.au/.

200 van Dooren, *Flight Ways,* 27–29.

CODA

1 Natasha Myers, "Edenic Apocalypse: Singapore's End-of-Time Botanical Tourism," in *Art in the Anthropocene,* ed. Heather Davis and Etienne Turpin (London: Open Humanities Press, 2005), 31.

2 Deborah Bird Rose, "Multispecies Knots of Ethical Time," *Environmental Philosophy* 9, no. 1 (2012): 130–31.

3 Peter Larkin, *Leaves of Field* (Exeter, U.K.: Shearsman, 2004), 45.

4 Rose, "Multispecies Knots of Evolutionary Time," 128.

5 W. H. Auden, *Selected Poems* (London: Faber, 1979), 82.

6 Seamus Heaney, *Finders Keepers: Selected Prose 1971–2001* (London: Faber, 2002), 189, 190.

Index

Species, 27–28. *See also* Bishop, Elizabeth
Davis, Heather, 74, 78
Dawkins, Richard, 47
deep time: the Anthropocene, 2, 5–7; arche-fossil, 39–40; deep future, 6, 13, 17, 22, 109, 120–22; evolutionary time, 9, 12, 25–28, 30, 55–56, 91, 121; fast and slow time, 16; genome, 109–10, 118–19; as gift, 29–30, 41, 91; history of, 9–10; life enfolded in, 9–10, 16–20, 25–48, 52–53, 73–74, 90–91, 94–95, 100–102, 106, 108–9, 127–28, 135n85; plastic and materiality of, 7, 53, 73–74, 78–83, 86; shallow time, 70, 83. *See also* extinction; kin-making
Deinococcus radiodurans, 13, 93, 108, 110, 112, 114, 118, 120, 122, 152n145
DeLanda, Manuel, 36
Derrida, Jacques, 28
Dibley, Ben, 7
Dickinson, Adam, 73; "Hail," 83
Dickinson, Emily, "Death Sets a Thing Significant," 116
diffraction, 12, 54–55, 58–59, 64, 68, 70, 74–75, 82, 97–98, 105. *See also* poetics: of diffraction
Diprose, Rosalyn, 43
DNA information storage, 108–9
Doty, Mark, "Difference," 13, 93, 96–98, 121–22, 128

ecocriticism: in the Anthropocene, 4–8, 20–22; criticism of, 4; history of, 3–5
Elder, John, 3
elegy, 84–85, 116, 122, 128;

anticipatory, 117, 120; ecological, 117, 119–20, 122
Eliot, T. S., 6
Ellsworth, Elizabeth, 18
epigenetic poetics, 113
ethical time, 12, 91
extinction, 7, 9, 12–13, 48, 75, 91–93, 98–101, 110, 116–17, 120–23, 127
extractivism, 9, 11, 20, 46, 53, 60, 73, 81, 126, 128

Fisher, Tom, 78–79, 81
flight ways, 12–13, 83, 91, 101, 103, 110, 121, 126
fossil fuels, 5, 10, 20, 47, 52, 68
Freud, Sigmund, 81
Frost, Robert, 61

Gaard, Greta, 3
Gabrys, Jennifer, 55, 75, 79, 81
Garrard, Greg, 3, 35
gene fetishism, 110–12
genome time, 109–10
geologic agency, 9, 16, 18
geologic intimacy, 9–10, 17–20, 29, 34, 37–38, 40–42, 47–48, 52, 127
geologic life, 10, 29–30, 40, 47
geophilia, 10, 18, 29
Gifford, Terry, 3, 62
Gilroy, Paul, 85
Ginn, Franklin, 93
Glotfelty, Cheryll, 3
Gordon, Avery, 120
Great Oxygenation Event, 7, 48
Green, Kelsey, 93
Greenblatt, Stephen, 89
Griffiths, Matthew, 6, 7
Grosz, Elizabeth, 10, 25, 28, 33–34
Guha, Ramachandra, 4

(continued from page ii)

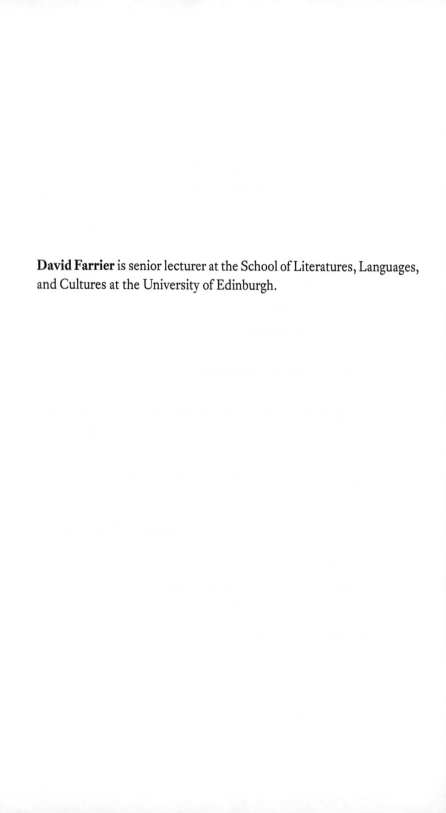

David Farrier is senior lecturer at the School of Literatures, Languages, and Cultures at the University of Edinburgh.